# An Apprenticeship
# in the School of Anxiety

## Jerry Januszewski

An Apprenticeship in the School of Anxiety
© 2019 Jerry Januszewski
Design: Jacco van der Ploeg, be-ink.nl
Print: Be Ink, Hoofddorp

ISBN: 978-0-578-43474-2


A publication of the Nanny MariaWilhelmina deVries
Foundation

*For the Ones Who Remember*

# Table of Contents

# PREFACE

The brilliant and influential Renaissance philosopher, and father of the modern essay, Michel de Montaigne, once remarked, "If my mind could gain a firm footing, I would not make essays, I would make decisions; but it is always in apprenticeship and on trial." For him, the curious, questioning, truth-seeking mind was ever moving forward, seeking something solid to stand on. Writing essays was his vehicle of inquiry, and his stance toward the truth was as an apprentice.

In the service of truth, everything in Montaigne's world was open to examination. He probed his own experience for universal principles in scrupulous and sometimes embarrassing detail. In all things his guiding principle was to love the truth and follow wherever it led. I desire to make his quest my own, which is why I am a frequent visitor to the greatest and most inspirational library in the world.

The United States Library of Congress in Washington, DC, is a man-made wonder — a sanctuary for the written word. The sublime inscriptions on the white marble walls of the Great Hall pay tribute to the highest thoughts of humankind in philosophy, religion, art, science, history, law and literature. One can read the walls there for hours without opening a single book.

The inscriptions even include thoughts about thoughts, as in this one attributed to Philipp Sydney: "They are never alone that are accompanied by noble thoughts." The sweet fellowship I feel in the company of books on my own shelves attest to this truth; books seem alive with the noble thoughts and personalities of their authors and in my ongoing interactions with them.

Religion and philosophy continue their stimulating conversation on the Library of Congress walls as the prophet Micah asks, "What doth the LORD require of thee, but to do justly, and to love mercy, and to walk humbly with thy God?" On another wall, the great scientist Francis Bacon adds, "The inquiry, knowledge, and belief of truth is the sovereign good of human nature."

I have a special affection for Francis Bacon because of another of his gems on the wall of the Great Hall that struck a deep chord of need in me and altered my life direction:

READING MAKETH A FULL MAN;

CONFERENCE A READY MAN;

AND WRITING AN EXACT MAN

I embraced Bacon's advice, which led me on an intellectual and spiritual journey that was at once more systematic and more mysterious than I knew before. I read the ideas of great authors, I conversed with kindred spirits about the ideas, and I wrote about the ideas with as much precision as I could. The essays collected in this volume map some of the terrain of that journey, written from 2009-2017.

I am often amazed at how a thought that seems lucid and complete in my mind appears sloppy and illogical once committed to the page; therefore, I read, discuss, and write some more. If I am steadfast in my effort, this cycle reliably produces a fullness, a readiness, and a clarity of mind and emotion that pleases me, even when that clarity involves difficult mental states such as anxiety or shame.

This is not a speedy process for me. Some of the essays here, though barely a thousand words in length, took several years to write, and far longer to live. I have needed to make peace with the incremental and idiosyncratic nature of my intellectual life and memory. As long as I apply Bacon's method of inquiry and determine, as Montaigne did, to love the truth wherever it leads, I experience a pleasurable expansion of the soul.

I hope your reading of these essays will create a fellowship between us by stimulating your thinking, allowing you a smile of recognition, and by helping you feel a little better about your present struggles.

Jerry Januszewski

# An Apprenticeship
# in the School of Anxiety

# 1

# The Beauty of Boredom

I'll never forget my father's reaction when he found me reading the magnificent *How to Read a Book* by Mortimer Adler. "You're reading a book about reading a book?" he asked in disbelief. "Diane!" he called to my mother. "Why did we ever take him out of Catholic school?" So I can forgive anyone for having the same dubious reaction as my father when I say one of the most exciting books I ever read is about boredom. *Boredom, Self and Culture* by Seán Desmond Healy helped me consolidate thoughts I'd had for years about the paradoxical devastation and beauty of boredom.

Most people trivialize the experience of boredom. Healy writes, "This supposedly commonplace perception of [boredom] as a virtual unavoidable occupational hazard, disagreeable but harmless, possessed even as it might be of redeeming educational value inasmuch as it prepares its victims for the greater boredom to come – a kind of educational vaccine stimulating the production of characteriological antibodies to contain future onslaughts."

If only it were that predictably beneficial. In reality, boredom is usually corrosive and destructive to the human personality. It is a major factor in the self-defeating behavior patterns that cause us all so much pain. And yet, within the experience of boredom resides the potential for self-knowledge leading to deep fulfillment.

Healy makes the distinction between simple boredom and hyper-boredom. Simple boredom comes from tedious activity, a reaction to a monotonous irritant. Hyper-boredom is a more serious deep-seated agony, rooted in a perception of inner emptiness. Simple boredom is a response to an external something. Hyper-boredom is a response to an internal nothing. It is this hyper-boredom, the true subject of Healy's book, that I take very seriously.

The experience of hyper-boredom is manifestly intolerable. Proof of this is found in how quickly, almost desperately, we seek to escape it. We feel bored, that is, empty, and almost instantly we take evasive action, doing just about anything to divert ourselves: text someone, use the computer, turn on music, eat, drink or smoke. Even fiddling with a pen will do. Almost any diverting activity is preferred to the perception of interior emptiness we euphemistically call boredom. The more keenly felt, the more assiduously avoided. Since hyper-boredom is so easily appeased without being truly remedied, we fail to recognize its controlling power.

As Healy notes, the common denominator of all hyper-boredom is the loss of personal meaning. The idea of life without meaningful purpose panics the soul. Many people are reluctant to examine this in a personal way; they may do so only with detached philosophic interest. Or they may avoid the subject altogether because personalizing the question makes it terrifying. If I sense emptiness in me, what does that say about who I am?

Fleeing the threat of personal meaninglessness through agreeable distractions might be a reasonable solution for simple boredom; simply fend off tedium with novelty. But the experience of hyper-boredom is deeper, chronic and not dissipated through mere amusement.

Hyper-boredom is largely metaphysical; experienced apart from sensory events. Seeking better distractions, more inventive and original experiences, may be sufficient to reduce simple boredom, but leaves aching hyper-boredom untouched.

This sheds light on why the pursuit of pleasure for pleasure's sake invariably results in boredom. We want the pleasure that thrills to continue thrilling indefinitely. But our response to the pleasure adapts, tolerance increases, what was novel becomes ordinary; the thrill is gone and we are left even more susceptible to hyper-boredom than before we started. If you like to drink, you might find that it now takes four beers to accomplish the buzz that used to come with two beers. This should concern you, not for fear of alcoholism, but for fear of your inner life becoming even more vulnerable to the existential yawn of hyper-boredom.

The redemptive potential of boredom exists in the possibility that the discomfort will drive us to devote honest attention to our souls' true need: its thirst for meaning, not distraction. What does my experience of emptiness reveal about my fears and my needs? Our inner unrest is a portal leading to answers to that question and more.

In Dante's *Inferno* the lost souls in Hell rushed to their judgement, desiring the very thing they feared. If we are to lay hold of Beauty begat of Boredom, we must confront the same inclination in our own souls to rush to the usual diversions that perpetuate the hellish hyper-boredom we fear. Avoiding the confrontation with our own emptiness leads to a greater, more protracted and painful struggle in the end.

How does one allow the experience of boredom to act as a guide? We decide to seek the examined life and begin asking ourselves questions: How do I divert myself when bored? What feeling am I trying not to feel through the diversion? Then we may cultivate a practice of "sitting" with the undistracted self instead of rushing to the diversion. Note the resistance felt. What is being resisted? The perception of nothing? Practice waiting it out until something emerges from the nothing, as it will in time.

This is the struggle, resisting the urge to flee to the pleasant distraction, and it takes courage. Try these questions when feeling nervous in a social situation: Why is the discomfort there? What feelings about the self are there? Are those feelings valid? What is the catastrophe I fear? How likely is that to happen in this situation? What better things could happen? As we progress in this kind of self-examination, we learn how enfeebling the distraction was and how invigorating this manner of self-discovery can be.

The perception of inner emptiness, what Seán Desmond Healy calls hyper-boredom, is not a nuisance but an invitation to a radical change in our approach to life. This inquisitive attitude towards boredom is counter-intuitive, ironic and yes, exciting.

# 2

# Stress and Wonder

W hen I arrived in the small city in southern India, I had high hopes for a relaxed sabbatical. My personal stress was high. I wanted one full year of rest so I could decide whether to continue in the addiction counseling profession. I admit that moving to India to relieve stress was a little extreme, but I felt my situation demanded a bold move, and this was it.

India is usually a difficult place to get things done. But to my surprise everything came together quickly. I rented an apartment and bought furniture, a stove, refrigerator, and water dispenser. I had my laptop computer and internet hook-up. There was a public pool nearby, a health club for working out, and even a basketball court. I purchased a cell phone for local use. Three boxes of my books sent from the U.S. arrived right on time. My stress reduction sabbatical in India was working out great so far.

Despite my need to avoid work tension, I couldn't help myself from investigating the local facilities for drug and alcohol treatment. How did they do things here in India? In a chance encounter I met the powerful chief administrator for a large western-style hospital, Mr. Peter. Typical of the friendly and generous spirit in India, Mr. Peter invited me to tour the hospital and meet his "top staff." I figured I'd be escorted from office to office, shaking hands with influential medical officials. I recall feeling like a big shot: self-satisfied with how well I was in control of my new challenges in this foreign land.

The morning of our scheduled appointment arrived. As I boarded a rickshaw for the ten-minute ride to the hospital, my new cell phone rang.

"Jeddy!" It was Mr. Peter. "Jeddy, the topic we'd like you to speak on today is stress reduction."

"What? Speak? I don't understand, Mr. Peter."

"Yes, your topic for our staff training today is stress reduction. Speak for as long as you like. Good-bye!" And he was gone with a click.

Minutes later I found myself standing at the front of a large conference room packed with doctors, nurses and hospital administrators. Dazed but trying to gather myself, I whispered to a nearby assistant, "Does everyone here speak English?" About half, was his reply. This did not diminish my stress.

I was introduced as "a top addictionologist from America." There was enthusiastic applause. A young nurse presented me with a bouquet of flowers. Everyone was smiling. I was still fumbling in my mind about what I was going to say. I couldn't have known it at the time, but this was the first of many encounters that year where I was spontaneously placed before a sea of Indian faces and expected to say something interesting.

One thing I learned from that experience: stress reduction is a popular topic, worldwide. In the United States and everywhere else I visited, almost everyone believes they have too much stress. We think a lot about what stresses us and we think a lot about how to rid ourselves of what stresses us. Despite all that thinking, human beings remain a stressed-out race.

What to do? Does facing stress effectively mean reducing or avoiding the unpleasant things that vex us? Is getting rid of unwanted stress as easy as moving to a new place? The answers may depend on whether we believe the stress has an interior or exterior origin.

Epictetus, the first-century philosopher, was a practical man who was very concerned with stress reduction. According to Epictetus, freedom from stress comes from a realistic acceptance of our natural limits. When we harbor anxiety, wishing to change an unpleasant situation that is out of our control, we are unfree, acting slavishly. Epictetus asserts that the source of all stress is interior, and therefore we have a great measure of control over our experience of stress.

When we allow ourselves to dwell with uncertainty, even embrace it, we transform stress into wonder. A sense of wonder opens wide our vision to the fascination and beauty in life. So much felt stress is unnecessary and can be restored to its rightful place in our hearts and minds as wonder.

My friend Epictetus, and international travel, taught me, not about stress reduction, but about stress transformation. Living in unfamiliar cultures is a wild ride, an adventure that shouldn't be, and truly can't be, completely controlled. When I chose to accept unforeseen changes and inconveniences as wondrous adventures, my stress level went way down. Much stress in life can be viewed the same way. To not do so and remain stressed, Epictetus says, is nothing but a failure of the imagination.

# 3

# Getting Drunk as a Rite of Passage

My first job as an addiction counselor was at a clinic in a housing project near Baltimore. It was a dangerous place to work because the drug trade was open and the police presence was insufficient. It wasn't uncommon to hear gunshots in the neighborhood at night.

The director of the clinic was just the kind of guy I needed: an experienced, street-wise counselor who was willing to take me, a suburban kid, under his wing. The closest I'd ever been to heroin addiction before then was watching movies about it. He and I would sit by a darkened window and watch drug transactions happening across the street from the clinic. He pointed out the crack cocaine users; they came and went several times through the evening. For the heroin users, one purchase was all they needed before vanishing into the night.

This criminal scene, while instructive, was very painful to watch. The drug buyers were subject to numerous humiliations, which I discovered were the inevitable outcome of addiction. And I learned that beyond the humiliation of addiction was death; and not very far beyond either.

How is one to understand this behavior, when the intense pursuit of a fading pleasure so predictably brings degradation with it? The substance users desired something, and they desired it more than they dreaded humiliation, more than they feared death. But what was it they desired? What was missing?

In natural and human ecology there are curious cyclical connections between death and renewal. Plants and animals die and become part of the soil that produces food for the living. One generation leaves resources for the next. Death precedes rebirth.

Human transformation is often understood as the old self being mortified in some fashion to allow the new self to emerge. Transformation rituals, rites of passage, are legitimate and necessary for healthy progress through the stages of life. This is often represented symbolically, as in baptism or graduation ceremonies. In authentic rites of passage, participants are willing to accept humiliation and perhaps risk death for passage into a higher way of life with a better self. If our culture fails to provide productive ways for us to find this renewal in a death-and-rebirth cycle, we seek it out ourselves in ways that are sometimes more destructive than renewing.

Drinking and drug use in college is spoken of by some as a rite of passage, allegedly aiding the transformation from youth to adulthood. The idea is that intoxication represents a sort of death, a passage into a transcendent state, from which the person returns changed in some important and useful way. In legitimate rites of passage, the participant goes through the death experience in order to receive a gift, after which he or she reenters society with a new and elevated social status, and with a new contribution to make.

The pursuit of intoxication does not accomplish this. It does provide the metaphoric death (transcendent separation from my sober self, entering into a substance using culture) without the subsequent returning to society with genuine, newly acquired gifts to offer. The substance user is seeking something ennobling in an ignoble way, destined to fail because the experience of intoxication eventually takes more than it gives.

A literal death came to the clinic where I worked. A patient who had been building a seemingly healthy recovery from heroin addiction, a guy who was an example and inspiration to other patients, died of a heroin overdose. I visited his family and loved ones who were dumbstruck by the news. I sat on the sofa in his mother's living room trying to console his best friend, but not knowing what to say. The friend described how well his buddy had been doing, how bright the future seemed, and how incomprehensible was his return to heroin use. Everything seemed to be going so well. In wide-eyed grief he looked at me and asked, "What was missing?"

What was missing? A tragic question when asked in the past tense. Of all the questions we ponder in life, this question, asked in the present tense, may be one of the most important. If heavy drinking and other drug use are supposed to be rites of passage to a better self by providing something that's missing, is the strategy succeeding? What is missing and what is gained? Without honest answers to those questions, authentic passage to our better selves is hindered.

# 4

# The Competitive Urge

The competitive urge is a curious phenomenon. At a social gathering I recall teaching my neighbor's eight-year-old son how to play the tabletop "football" game. This involves each player taking turns pushing a coin across the table. Getting the coin to hang over the edge of the table without falling off is a "touchdown."

The boy was excited to learn the game and he immediately wanted to play against me. I played with restraint and allowed him to win the game. The moment he hit the winning shot, his eyes lit up, he jumped straight into the air and shouted, "I am champion! I am champion!" — to the great amusement of the other kids and adults crowding around us to watch the contest. We played a second game and this time I was less generous. As I aimed the potential winning shot, I paused to consider the emotional impact on the boy. How would he handle losing his "championship" in front of everyone? I considered intentionally missing the shot, but I didn't want to lose to him twice, so I went for the win and got it.

To my surprise the boy's eyes lit up again and he jumped up into the air just as before, this time shouting, "You are second champion! I am first champion!" Our competitive urges, his and mine, were curious indeed.

I came from a family well acquainted with competitive sports. My father and my mother were coaches who believed in the noblest aspects of sports. They made it clear that they wanted me to play for the love of the game and to be a good sportsman: humble in victory and gracious in defeat.

I professed agreement with their ethic, but deep down I didn't embrace it. In certain ways I was a coach's dream: a cooperative, hard-working player who never gave up. I wanted to win, or so I thought. But, while I was glad to perform well, winning was not nearly as satisfying as I expected it to be. I discovered I was ambitious for something else. I didn't want merely to win; I wanted to feel superior to my opponent. In high school basketball games, I would stare at my adversary with real contempt; I considered him beneath me. Even on my own team it mattered to me, not only that I worked hard, but also that I worked harder than everyone else. I hated to lose to anyone. I hated to lose far more than I valued winning.

Losing represented painful inferiority, and a hate-to-lose approach to achievement used my fear of feeling inferior to motivate higher performances. This seemed to work for me at first, helping me push for the extra effort that sometimes was the difference between victory and defeat.

But a hate-to-lose mentality as a motivator became a problem because it made winning incidental and eventually irrelevant. When not-losing is more important than everything else, then everything else, such giving your best effort or winning, are no longer the point of playing. For me winning became only a postponement of self-doubt that would arise the next time I needed to compete again and defend against a new assault of inferiority.

What was worse, I knew plenty of coaches who actively advocated the hate-to-lose approach. With contorted faces and impassioned voices, they'd tell the team that to succeed as an athlete, "You gotta HATE to LOSE!" This mentality is very prevalent on all levels of sport, from pee-wees to the pros.

The negative effects are subtle at first, obscured by the performance benefits. Eventually, though, that mindset produces fear-driven athletes who have lost their first love of the game.

This perplexed and depressed me. I avoided sports for a while, but something drew me back into the game. Eventually I developed an understanding of athletics that was transformative for me in other areas of life as well.

At the core of this issue for me is the struggle for self-definition, for an answer to the question "Who am I?" An alternative approach to the fear-based comparison game involves abandoning the competitive urge as a primary source of motivation for that self-definition. This means embracing a mindset of self-discovery that's not dependent in any way on one's relative rank to other human beings. This approach is very hard to do, and is so foreign a way of thinking to most that it is often ridiculed as weak, foolish or unambitious.

Struggle and striving are still necessary – the ranking as a basis for identity is not. It is essential to encounter resistance from forces larger than ourselves that challenge us in ways we can't fully control or predict.

The self-definition born of true knowledge of our absolute limitations is, paradoxically, freeing. Freeing, in part, because it allows us to identify with others instead of comparing with others.

Identification with others based on our common limitations enables us to love them rather than see them as competitors, and therefore threats. The fear of losing vanishes in this approach because in this way resistance and loss become the teachers that propel us far higher than the conventional ideas of competitive success.

Seen this way, true humility is cultivated, not of lowliness, but of equality. Humility is a freedom from slavish comparisons with others.

Stepping out of this hierarchical way of thinking is frightening, which is why it is far easier to think in a competitive way to justify ourselves. The competitive urge as a basis for our sense of self is a calamity. The day we stop trying to justify ourselves through comparison with others may be one of the greatest days of our lives.

# 5

# I Can't Stay Mad at You

My sister Bonnie and I are only one year apart but she was much taller than I was for most of our childhood. Her size and stature as the eldest sibling meant that I followed her lead in most things. I wanted to go to kindergarten because Bonnie went to kindergarten. I wanted to read books because Bonnie read books. She protected me from neighborhood bullies and gave me tissues for my runny nose. Observing Bonnie and copying how she did things is how I faced most childhood challenges.

At times I resisted her directives. We'd fight, but eventually I'd give in to her way because I was no match for her superior powers of argumentation. A good example of this was the piggy bank incident.

We were both given plastic piggy banks. I was a more diligent saver than Bonnie, so I accumulated an enviable amount of change. One day Bonnie said, "Jerry, if we take all the money in your piggy bank and put it in my piggy bank, we'll have a lot more money!" Dazzled by her logic, I spent an entire morning using a butter knife to extract the coins from my piggy bank; coins which Bonnie immediately deposited into her bank. How excited I was to shake Bonnie's piggy bank, to feel its massive weight and hear the deep, full-bodied resonance of our combined fortunes.

Days later, when I encountered the soulless shell of what was my piggy bank and realized I had no money, I became outraged and went to Bonnie demanding my money back. But I was too late. She had already spent the entire sum on a ceramic ash tray—a gift for our dear mother for Mother's Day.

Bonnie was shrewd, but she was also generous. Giving, not taking, was her ultimate goal. Weeks before she had noticed the ash tray in the window of a beauty parlor near our house and devised her plan to procure it. That plan happened to require the contents of my piggy bank.

As Bonnie explained to me her motives, I was bewildered. This was the first time it occurred to me that I could or should do anything sacrificial for my mother, who was there, it seemed to me, to do things for me. But it wasn't the first time this idea occurred to Bonnie. She was always thinking about others with kindness. True, she tricked me out of my savings, but Bonnie was a noble trickster. I marvel now at how considerate a person she was at age six. How fortunate I was to have her example, then and now, for how to live generously in the world.

Growing up with Bonnie taught me to be suspicious of my initial reactions, because they often misled me about the higher benefits of a situation. I wanted to stay mad at Bonnie for filching my cash, but I couldn't hold a grudge when I saw how touched my mother was with her present. "It's from me and Jerry," Bonnie was quick to explain. Nope, I couldn't stay mad at Bonnie.

Living generously in the world is a fruit of the well examined life. It's a life lived deliberately in service of others: offering gifts instead of demanding payment. In our society of conspicuous consumption, it would be normal to approach daily interactions with a consumer mentality. But we are here to contribute something as well, which, in my mind, involves living generously like Bonnie.

Living generously is difficult in a world where it seems our anger is provoked daily. We're angry when we don't beat the red light and we're angry when people don't love or respect us the way we long to be loved and respected. A particular brand of white-hot anger is reserved for political discourse informed by the idea that some other person or group is taking something away that is rightfully ours. In politics, kindness is often regarded as weakness. How does one live generously in this kind of world?

The noted psychologist Carl Jung said, "The will to power and the will to love are mutually exclusive; when one is present, the other is absent." Generosity thrives where there is the will to love. As long as we value love over power, we pursue the generous path. To pursue power over love is to declare cynicism the victor.

The ceramic ash tray Bonnie purchased was not technically beautiful, but it originated from her will to love and that made it valuable as gold. If we interact with this spirit instead of a competitive, self-serving one, it's quite possible an agreeable sweetness will enter our inner lives, as our anger becomes useless and then vanishes.

When we meet others' vulnerability with warmth, meaningful moments of connection can occur. We see with greater clarity how our initial impulse to maneuver for our own advantage or defense can lead us away from meaningful experience. Life changes when we trust the will to love. Or rather, we change. We form a new relationship with life—life as it is—to which we can say, even in hard times, "I can't stay mad at you."

# 6

# Shame and the Examined Life

It's easy to think of Socrates' famous call to live the examined life as a masculine endeavor. I've seen *The unexamined life is not worth living* tattooed on a man's arm, I've heard it in locker room speeches, and I've felt its inspiring tug on my own soul. A well-known line from *Hamlet* is similarly evocative: "This above all: to thine own self be true, and it must follow, as the night the day, thou canst not then be false to any man."

These heroic sentiments can make even a hardened man shed a tear, as he recognizes a worthy First Principle. But desiring the examined life is one thing, actually living it is another.

Years ago, I worked for an addiction treatment program at the county jail. Inmates frequently tested me for my "street cred" (of which I had none). Some of the cops working there hassled me as well. Word got out I had studied philosophy, and this added to the perception I was bookish, with no street smarts.

This work situation exposed to me some of my hidden shame: doubts I had about whether I was man enough to deal with real life tough guys. So I searched for ways to prove my manly mettle to the others, even as I doubted I had any. When I was invited to train alongside the cops in some of their special maneuvers, I was eager to do it. Now here was something in my wheelhouse, I thought: running and jumping and generally being athletic. I'm going to show those cops a thing or two!

We were taken to a huge structure with no windows that simulated the dark interior of a building on fire. Inside was a crazy labyrinth through which each of us were expected to crawl, feeling our way through the pitch-dark with our hands.

I was keenly aware all the cops were watching when I took my turn. It didn't go well. With a big oxygen tank on my back, I could barely move through the claustrophobic crawl-space. The twists and turns were designed to disorient the mind, and within sixty seconds I wasn't sure which way was up. There were dead-ends, which meant I had to inch my way out backwards. This I did, but sometimes into another dead-end. My hands searched for an acceptable opening in any direction. My throat felt choked. They had warned me: control your breathing or else fear will get the best of you.

Fear did get the best of me and I banged on the wall: the signal for rescue needed. Hidden doors opened and in a few seconds I felt a hand on my collar pulling me out. Outside the building I ripped off the oxygen mask and gulped fresh air. I was drenched in sweat, my hands shaking. My audience of cops thought this was hilarious. I felt humiliated; my shame, I thought, in full view to those I sought to impress. I wanted to quit, but after gathering my emotions, I forced myself to try again.

Going back into that dark, stifling hot building was one of the hardest things I ever did. But my resistance to do it was not because of the ordeal of completing the maze, difficult as that was. I was desperate to avoid placing myself in a position, once again, where my personal shame—not being man enough — was exposed by my failure. This has everything to do with the difficulty of living the examined life.

There is an unavoidable ambivalence connected to the path of self-discovery. We're drawn to the unexplored within and also frightened by it. The poet James Russell Lowell asked, "Who's not sat tense before his own heart's curtain?" Accepting the call to an examined life is heroic, because it takes courage to go beyond fear of our suspected insufficiencies to the freedom of full self-acceptance. Refusing the call means remaining, in some sense, a slave to fear. The philosopher Eva Brann goes further, noting that the unexamined life is not merely not worth living, but it is already dead: "...the unsearched-out life is unlivable....you're a grey shade, in Hades before your time," she writes.

Considering our attraction to the examined life, and the dreadful consequences of refusing the call, why does fear so easily hinder us from seeking and embracing our true and free selves? One explanation concerns this experience of human shame I've just described for myself, but which is likely common to all.

Shame feelings are a torment to the soul. If self-examination threatens to reveal agonizing shame, then resistance to this process begins to make sense. Felt shame is an enemy to personal freedom because it squashes the impulse for the examined life.

Dr. Ernest Kurtz, in his concise and brilliant book *Guilt and Shame* states that both guilt and shame involve feeling "bad" about something. They differ in that we feel a pang of guilt over something we do, but we feel the ache of shame over something we are. Shame is the perception of an ugly flaw within our own being, an inherent defect that makes us uniquely worse than other people. We may feel embarrassed because someone sees our misdeeds (guilt), but we feel humiliated when someone sees our shame. So we go to great lengths to hide our shame from others and from ourselves.

Often, we develop a mental image of an ideal self, a comforting version of ourselves we imagine without the shame, which we also present to the world. This is an understandable strategy for suppressing shame feelings, but a deeply flawed one for pursuing the examined life.

Despite feeling enormous resistance, I attempted the dark maze again and this time I controlled my breathing better. After 15 minutes of steady progress, I reached the end and emerged into the sunshine. Again, I ripped my mask off, this time in triumph, but there wasn't a single cop there to witness my victory, except for the trainer supervising my effort. They'd all gone in for lunch.

I'm grateful now that none of the cops were there to see me complete the maze successfully, because that gave me the opportunity to wrestle with my internal shame, not my superficial embarrassment. The examined life demanded I honestly face how I felt about myself, apart from any observer. Facing this shame was much harder, and much more fruitful, than merely proving something to others.

This was a turning point for me for examining my true self and finding some freedom in the examined life – a call that is neither exclusively masculine nor feminine, but human.

# 7

# Sowing the Seeds of Civilization

Picture yourself walking alone on a path leading to your home or job. Up ahead you see another person walking in your direction, someone with whom you're not acquainted. You are two strangers passing each other and you feel mildly conflicted. A normal inclination to offer a polite hello is hindered by felt shyness, a natural introversion or an understandable wariness of potential predators. "Be cool, be cool," you tell yourself as you affect a nonchalant manner. You may or may not say hello. If you do, the other person may or may not acknowledge your greeting. For such a commonplace awkward experience, it's curious there are no standard, explicit instructions about it in the accepted rules of conduct for our culture.

If this tendency towards shyness, privacy or suspicion pervades smaller communities, whose cultural health is dependent on a network of trusting personal relationships, then an isolating chill can settle upon human interactions in that community. An experience as unexceptional as saying hello to a fellow solitary walker and receiving no reply can produce an acute feeling of disconnect. What is the long-term effect if we experience this regularly?

A study published in the *Journal of Affective Disorders* followed more than a thousand students through their college years. The researchers determined one of the most reliable predictors of suicidal thoughts was a lack of social support: feeling unappreciated and isolated from family and friends.

The persistent feeling of isolation cited by many college students may seem surprising, considering how potential friendships abound in the college scene. But the path to true intimacy in friendships is not as clear-cut as one might assume. Individuals within a polity almost unconsciously seek to overcome isolation through communal emotional experiences. These are traditions and group activities where everyone feels the same thing at the same time, for example, spectating at sporting events.

One could argue that the culture of drinking attempts to create communal emotions. Shared mood-altering experiences may level the emotional playing field, in a sense. We're gratified when we feel something together.

A simple greeting can accomplish a kind of emotional leveling as well. A sincere well-wishing between two human beings is a surprisingly potent way to momentarily bridge the isolation gap, to impart appreciation and sow the seeds of goodwill and trust in a community. We behold the face of another and we communicate with intention, however briefly. The implicit message of a greeting is *I respect your place in our community and I wish you well.* When shared, that's a lot of goodwill packed into a simple hello.

My father was a teacher and a master of the warm greeting. A student once confessed, with gratitude, that he intentionally walked out of his way in the school hallways each day, just so he could be greeted by my father. In the realm of good deed doing, a warm hello is vastly underrated.

In Book VII of *The Politics*, Aristotle contends that the integrity of a state depends on its citizens having a certain level of familiarity with each other. Aristotle advocates a limit of the total population of a state because its members function best when they have a reasonable trust level with a large percentage of members. French social commentator Alexis de Tocqueville, in his landmark *Democracy in America*, describes a distinctive American version of Aristotle's blueprint for a thriving civil society. We tend to form small associations around political, social and religious interests that manifest this familiarity and interdependent trust.

But something in this arrangement is breaking down. The isolated college student is not a singular phenomenon. There is a culture-wide trend away from individuals forming trusting relationships through organized affiliations, involving face-to-face interactions with others, unmediated by electronics. The average American is more isolated than in decades past, has fewer close friends and, presumably, experiences less goodwill.

Therefore, I have a very modest proposal for decisive action to increase the trust on a personal level: let's voluntarily greet one another when we have the opportunity to do so, instead of passing by in silence. A simple hello is all it takes to sow the seeds of civilized goodwill.

I don't wish to create any guilt around this for anyone. There's no compulsion. An individual may rightly maintain silence for his or her own valid privacy concerns. A greeting may in fact be ill-advised to carry out in crowded locales. Neither do I envision wearying anyone with perfunctory greetings carried out in the same way in the same places every day.

There is, however, much room for improvement. A personal greeting exchanged with the warmth we really feel over our shared humanity and our common love for our communities is a great equalizer and affirms the civil, egalitarian spirit we profess as Americans. I suspect even a small increase in face-to-face connectedness could make a positive difference. Will an increase of simple greetings end all estrangement, loneliness or even suicidal leanings? Not likely. This is why I call this idea a very modest proposal. But in its modesty lies its unassuming beauty: the power of small, incremental change.

Increasing the trust benefits everyone because we are all

nurtured by small reminders that we belong to a community and that we matter to others in it. The warm greeting is a lost art and a relatively easy way to make the world a better, more civilized place.

# 8

# The Legendary Arthur Mallamo

A forty-year-old memory occurred to me while I was attending a lecture about the effects of alcohol on the brain, presented by a professor of neurology from Johns Hopkins University. As I listened to the lecture and took notes, my mind drifted to my friendship with the legendary Arthur Mallamo.

Mr. Mallamo was my seventh-grade gym teacher. He was also a poet, a philosopher and a comedian. He had an intimidating presence and pushed-in, twisted nose that led to much speculation among us boys about how its unique shape was acquired. Theories ranged from him being a professional wrestler to a Mafia hit man. The truth was even more remarkable: he was a World War II bomber and fighter pilot who'd been shot down not once, but twice, and eluded capture both times. His misshapen nose was a reminder of his ordeals.

If Mr. Mallamo liked you, his way of showing it was to tease you in front of the class. One cold November day he had us running around the track, our thin gym uniforms providing almost no protection from the icy winds. As Mr. Mallamo exhorted us onward he bellowed, "Whoever comes in last has to take Januszewski home for Thanksgiving dinner!" It was then I knew we were getting along well.

He was also my health class teacher, which was where he expounded on various life lessons. He'd speak earnestly to us about living generously and about the value of dedicating your life to service. "Gentlemen," he'd say softly, "greed is a terrible thing."

One day a boy smuggled a very dead but otherwise intact frog into the classroom. As soon as Mr. Mallamo's back was turned, the boy, in a display of boldness I will always admire, launched the frog into the air like a grenade. It landed with an inert thud on the teacher's desk.

All eyes were on Mr. Mallamo as he turned, carefully examined the frog and said, "Gentlemen, this... is a frog. Am I going too fast for you, Januszewski?" We howled with laughter and loved him for that.

Another day in health class Mr. Mallamo explained how alcohol rendered brains cells less and less functional. To illustrate his point, he took the blackboard eraser in his huge hand and dangled it at arm's length.

"Gentlemen, this is what alcohol does to brain cells," and he dropped the eraser onto the desk surface, which sent a puff of chalk dust into the air. I got the message: drink too much and your brain cells go poof. This seemed plausible but was it true?

The neurology lecture at Johns Hopkins jogged my memory about Mr. Mallamo's lessons. It turns out that yes, alcohol, and drunkenness in particular, has a significant negative impact on an aspect of brain development called myelination.

Myelin is the material that forms a protective sheath around nerve cells, or neurons, enabling them to communicate and be social with each other. Proper myelination is vital for the cerebral cortex, the part of your brain that helps you succeed intellectually. Healthy myelination is very good for the gray matter: it enhances crisp thinking and efficient recall in our mental processes. Like people, neurons work well when they are well connected with each other.

One reason drinking is such an effective way to get high is that alcohol easily penetrates the myelin sheath to mess with cell function. The more intense the drinking, the more destructive the assault on the myelin sheath. If the myelination process is impaired, intellectual activity is also impaired; neurons become more rigid, less fluid, more easily irritated.

Poorly myelinated neurons work less efficiently, become poorer communicators and eventually die of loneliness. In practical terms, impaired myelination makes it harder to remember things, harder to concentrate, easier to be frustrated with new information. You could say a well myelinated brain is better able to enjoy exercising its intellect and a less well myelinated brain will struggle more.

Healthy myelination is important at all ages, but, according to the Johns Hopkins neurologist, the cerebral cortex in the human brain desires a myelination "growth spurt" in the 18-21 age range. The worst way to drink, from a brain growth perspective, is to binge drink in college. That's high-impact toxicity.

Once again, I tip my hat to my old gym teacher and friend, Arthur Mallamo. He was right to suggest that alcohol can diminish brain power well after we've finished drinking. If we value the life of the mind, it makes sense to examine how our drinking pleasures influence our intellectual pleasures. If there was a conflict between the two, which pleasure would take priority?

If you're mindful of how much you desire your intellectual powers to flourish and would like to limit your drinking, then the next time you're at a social gathering and someone offers you a drink, take the Johns Hopkins Neurologist's advice and feel free to say, "No thanks, I'm myelinating today."

# 9

# Learning from Lepers

One of the most gruesome and intriguing books I've ever read was written by a British physician who specialized in treating medical conditions commonly referred to as leprosy. In *Pain: The Gift Nobody Wants*, Dr. Paul Brand tells the poignant story of a young man named Raman, a patient at his clinic in India.

Raman's leprosy, rightly called Hansen's Disease, rendered him utterly insensitive to physical pain. Desensitized to injury, "lepers" are extra susceptible to wounds, infections and gross disfigurements of the skin and other features. The social stigma and practical difficulties of treating this condition are so formidable that many patients lose hope and stop complying with treatment. These despairing souls are true outcasts, occupying the lowest social stratum of any society they live in.

Raman, as Dr. Brand noted, possessed the courage and diligence to comply with the medical program. As his hands responded to treatment and became more dexterous, he experienced an expanded sense of self, giving him great hope for the future. He was eventually certified negative for leprosy.

Even though he still couldn't feel pain in his hands, they were functional. If he was careful to maintain his visual self-examination discipline, he would do fine. He went back to his hometown, eager to show the family that had ostracized him that he was all better.

Two days later Raman returned to the clinic completely defeated, with his hands bandaged. Despite his best efforts, both hands had been severely damaged on consecutive nights. One hand was gouged by a rat that had eaten his flesh while he slept, and the other hand had burned when it fell against a hot lamp, also while he slept. In deep despair, Raman, once he could speak about it, exclaimed, "I feel like I've lost all my freedom... how can I ever be free without pain?"

The perception of pain, known as nociception, is essential for developing the physical and emotional boundaries that allow all of us to survive in the world. Without it, human beings descend into a nightmare of painless confusion, emotional contraction and isolation. The experience of pain is both universal and intensely personal. When another person understands our pain, we're soothed because we feel less isolated. When another dismisses our pain as insignificant, we may feel humiliated. Understandably then, we disdain the experience of pain and react cautiously, even cynically, towards its proffered lessons about who we are and what connects us with our fellows.

Strange as it may seem, we need the instructive realities of pain to not only warn us of danger and injury, but to bring definition to our identities: our sense of where we end and the world begins, physically and emotionally. This is one way our suffering can be redemptive: being attentive to its lessons brings not only physical welfare but also emotional safety. Making the pain go away without gleaning the fruit of self-knowledge squanders the opportunity to trade misery for insight and freedom.

When a leprosy patient has no sensation in the limbs, an unfortunate psychological shift may take place. The patient's sense of his physical self contracts; it no longer includes the parts he cannot feel or use well. When the use of limbs is restored, a delightful emotional expansion takes place. That which the patient regards as his "self" has grown and is more available to him.

Our emotional lives are similarly connected to this dynamic of expansion or contraction. When we recognize and accept the full range of our emotional experience, especially the emotions that are unpleasant or shameful to us, then more of our emotional selves becomes available to us, and our inner lives are pleasingly expanded. When we do things to avoid, repress, or blunt emotions we don't approve of, we experience a contraction of our inner lives. Fear-driven behavior, depression, anxiety and addiction involve contracted inner states, often leading to greater isolation.

This hints at the curious relationship between human limits and freedom. Within healthy physical and emotional boundaries, a human being grows, thrives and expands, as seen in child rearing. Without healthy boundaries, a human personality becomes distorted, as with a tyrant who has no restraints on his behavior.

A life without pain is a life without limits. A life without limits is unhealthy and undesirable, sad and sometimes monstrous, and always tragic. I'm not arguing that we deliberately seek out pain. Life itself doles out quite enough struggle for all of us to learn essential lessons about ourselves. But what a sweet relief it is to draw a truce with our pain, when we're ready to do so, and be inquisitive about what it says about our places in the world.

When we discover that pain, though terrible, is also a gift-giver, then all our experience becomes imbued with meaning. This is one of the exquisite consolations of philosophy.

# 10

# The Anxiety Club

One warm September day in 1998, five of us from St. John's College went for a swim in the Chesapeake Bay at a beach about ten miles from campus. It was so much fun we kept going back, even into October. We were pleased with ourselves, swimming in what we thought was pretty cold water. It may have ended there, but then someone asked, "Why don't we swim outdoors every month of the school year?" Feeling flush with hope or hubris, we formalized our agreement. The St. John's College Polar Bear Club was born.

The air temperatures that November were balmy. It was 65 degrees the day we took our third plunge as a group. The water was cold, but not cold enough to keep us from laughing as we swam around. The swim felt like a great achievement. At dinner that evening we exchanged knowing glances, as if we were soldiers who survived combat together.

For some reason we were in no rush to get our December swim accomplished. As the temperatures began to drop, someone would say in passing, "Hey, we should get our swim in before it gets real cold." But we kept putting it off.

Christmas came and went, and still no swim. Everyone was still in town, so a meeting of the Polar Bear Club was called to order. The air temperature was now consistently around freezing, 32 degrees. Mary, our leader, pointed out we were in serious danger of failing our mission as an organization and also of invalidating any previous claim to toughness. Dave, our Second-in-Command, objected, asserting that swimming in this weather could lead to death. Mary and Dave were dating, and I thought I noticed a contentious glare exchanged between them.

My anxiety about whether to take the icy swim made me unusually passive about the decision. We all deferred to Mary and she determined we would swim the next day, December 31st at 6pm at the same beach. New Year's Eve – this was not quite the 11th hour, but it was awfully close.

The next evening we piled into my car and headed out to the beach. The mood was subdued, a far cry from our earlier swims. Outside it was 24 degrees, with wind gusts up to 20 mph. The normally tranquil beach had waves as big as ocean surf. It was dark and as uninviting a setting for swimming as you can imagine. We stood on the beach, shivering in our bathing suits and winter coats, huddled tightly to protect against the wind.

We argued again about whether we should risk this. Mary was for it. Dave was against it. I was wavering. I wanted Mary and Dave to be my mommy and daddy and tell me what to do. It was so cold.

Finally, Mary took charge, ripping off her furry coat and shouting, "I don't care! I'm going in!" She sprinted to the water and dove in. I mechanically followed her into the water. One of the others followed me in. Dave and one other member remained on the beach.

When you plunge into water that cold, two things happen in an instant. First, your body heat gathers to your body's core, which leaves your outer body, from head-to-toe, throbbing in pain. Even your face hurts. Second, panic takes over. The rational mind shuts down, except for one thought: MUST GET OUT NOW. To linger in the water after the initial shock of submersion would take an unnatural resolve.

We emerged from the water, screaming. But then a wonderful thing happened. Within 15 seconds of leaving the water, our body heat rushed back out to our skin and limbs. This produced an ecstatic sense of well-being. We stood on the beach without our coats, laughing, warm and happy and feeling, most amazing of all, a sweet absence of anxiety. That moment remains one of my fondest memories: a transformation of a high-anxiety moment into a magical one.

Later when I pondered this peak experience, I was dismayed at how my anxiety had incapacitated me; how passive I had felt in the face of the decision to swim or not. The philosopher Soren Kierkegaard said, "Anxiety is the dizziness of freedom." If he is correct, then the human inclination to escape anxiety could very well be an attempt to escape from freedom. A desire to escape anxiety by escaping freedom; did that explain my passivity?

One could argue that polar bear swimming is a frivolous activity. But my anxiety was real and dizzying because real freedom was involved. I had two choices, swim or not swim, and both were painful. Saying "I wanted Mary and Dave to be my mommy and daddy" was a wisecrack perhaps, but on that beach, I dearly wanted them to choose for me. All it took for me to be willing to forfeit my freedom of choice was a certain sufficient level of anxiety. This is frightening and it contradicted what I thought I stood for in the pursuit of a free life.

Our society regards anxiety as an enemy to happiness, not an ally. It feels so good to make anxieties disappear that there is widespread sympathy for removing them through almost any means, such as prescribed medications, alcohol and, increasingly, marijuana. I understand that sometimes incapacitating anxiety requires direct intervention. But I wonder how often we slavishly blunt anxiety to flee the "dizziness of freedom." What disturbing irony it would be if activities we pursue in the name of freedom, may in truth accomplish a flight from freedom.

Examining the origins of anxiety may reveal our present needs that are unfamiliar to us, but still deeply felt. What a rich source of self-knowledge is that state, if we can learn to tolerate it. For freedom's sake, are we willing to attend to our anxiety and learn its lessons instead of blotting it out? What if the resolve to do so is unnatural? Would that mean that, for all our talk about cherishing personal freedom, we are more inclined to choose comfort and security?

Embracing freedom means facing our anxiety with courage and curiosity, when everything inside us would rather flee that encounter. This is one of many fascinating and fruitful entrances to the well examined life, and the well examined society for that matter.

# 11

# The Discovery

My first alcoholic drink changed my life. It was the summer of my 14th year. Our town church held a festival every July called The Feast of St. Anthony. The Feast was not so much a religious event, but a raucous carnival; the kind where the normal rules of conduct were loosened.

At a booth I managed to knock down the milk cans with a baseball, and the grown-up running the booth, a classmate's father, put a bottle of wine in my hands. Normally he would never have given me alcohol, but this was The Feast, so even though I shouldn't have been surprised, I was startled to now be the owner of this cool, mysterious bottle. I cradled it in my arm like a football and hurried through the crowd to find my two close friends. After hacking through the cork with a pen knife, the three of us drank the whole bottle.

A happy, rosy glow overtook me. "Oh, I get it now," I said to my friends. "This is why people drink." Until that moment it had never entered my mind to seek out alcohol. If you asked me what I did for fun I would have said going to the beach, sports and reading. I didn't know such elevated emotions were available to me. This wasn't merely an insight, but a discovery.

I was confused by the phenomenon of drinking alcohol because it seemed mostly negative, making grown-ups I respected act stupidly. I was embarrassed for them when they drank. Stupid was the one thing I knew I didn't want to be. But now, having felt the buzz, I determined that the next chance I had to drink alcohol, I would do it.

That moment came about two years later at age 16. A recently graduated high school friend was able to sneak me into a college bar. The drinking age was 18 then. He bought me a beer and then left me alone as he went off to talk with other people he knew. I stood off to the side and surveyed this bar scene in wide-eyed wonder. People were happy and having fun, great music was playing, and there were pretty girls everywhere. Did that one just smile at me? This was awesome. I drank my beer like water.

Pretty soon my friend came by. "Hey JJ, you gotta nurse that beer along. Don't drink it fast." He bought me another. I felt manly, thinking I had found an essential ingredient for a life I would really love. The bar scene added a thrilling social dimension to the buzz. Whatever made me feel like an awkward outlier in life ceased to exist in the festive drinking scene, as long as I drank. So I sought it out whenever I could. Even when people started reporting back to me idiotic things I said or did the night before, I thought the drinking was worth it. Yes, I winced when told how I annoyed people with my argument about the merits of disco, and I didn't even like disco. And yes, I was mortified when I woke up on my friend's sofa, having passed out and pissed on it. And no, I didn't like having to apologize for my obnoxious behavior the day after some heavy drinking. But drinking was great, right?

Fast forward to age 21. I was at a bar with my buddies, six of us. We were good friends and knew each other well, or so I thought. There were three pitchers of beer on the table. As I refilled the cups around the table, the guy next to me, Harry, said no thanks.

"Not drinking tonight?" I asked.

"No, I never drink," he said. I was surprised.

"What do you mean you don't drink?"

"I don't drink." "Why not?"

"I don't care for it," he said.

I was amazed that I had been out in bars and at parties with Harry many dozens of times and I never realized he wasn't drinking right along with the rest of us. Just because someone at a social event has a cup in his hand, doesn't mean he has alcohol in the cup, I learned.

Ridicule is often a form of questioning and so even though I was curious, I poked fun at Harry at the time. Secretly, I admired him for being so self-assured, for following his own star. The truth was I didn't feel comfortable with the way I drank, but I lacked the self-possession and wherewithal to follow my own star, or even see it.

You may be expecting me to say how I eventually stopped drinking and found a better way of life. I did find a better way to manage my emotions, and that did involve "breaking up" with alcohol, in a sense. But the road to honest examination of myself — who I was, what I wanted, and why my life mattered — was more complex than deciding I no longer wanted to use drinking as a spiritual and social crutch. I now see that from the beginning I was on a path of discovery, but for me that path led far beyond the primitive and unmanly bounds of seeking to get "buzzed."

My path had to do not only with the large questions of truth, goodness and beauty, but also with everyday questions such as, "How can I comfortably interact with people and still be myself?" and "Why do I care so much about what others think of me?" and simply, "What makes a good day good?" Drinking became a hindrance to me, so I merely chose to take alcohol out of the equation as I sought answers to those compelling questions.

# 12

# Your Sex Life on Porn

Once I was invited to the off-campus home of some male college students. As I approached the front door, I could see through an opening in the curtain of the large picture window. The TV was on and they were watching a porn film. I knocked on the door and prepared myself for an awkward moment. When they opened the door and brought me inside, I was relieved to see the TV was off.

While pornography is attractive to men as ever, gone are the days of taking social risks in public to obtain sexually explicit material. The Internet has reduced the social and economic hindrances of procuring porn films to near zero. I read that 30 percent of women and 70 percent of men admit to ever having viewed online porn. My informal inquiries indicate that for college students, that number is closer to 100 percent for both genders. A significant percentage of those students assert that viewing porn is a positive and healthy activity.

For many boys, porn was their introduction to sex education. Naturally curious about the mechanics of sex, boys find basic answers in porn. Porn also indoctrinates viewers with an ethos about relationships, intimacy and the self. Most men view porn long before their first real sexual encounter. By the time a man engages in sexual activity with another person, he has likely received hundreds, if not thousands, of images into his psyche of other human bodies having sex.

Even if watching online porn is now the norm, we do well to ask if viewing porn is healthy for the sex lives of men and women. Do these films provide essential knowledge that leads to satisfying sexual relationships?

We all agree viewing porn can be a powerful experience. But being moved by something is not sufficient proof of its goodness, as Aristotle cautions us in his *Nicomachean Ethics*. How does one make a clear-eyed assessment of the overall effect of porn on a human being?

The desire for sex is primal and mind-bending. Jokes are legion about how the sex drive can distort a person's rational powers. We chuckle in agreement when we hear comedian Robin Williams' line, "God gave man a brain and a penis — but not enough blood to use them both at the same time." Add the effects of alcohol consumption, and sexual self-governance can be nonexistent. I've known many who were wounded by such situations.

No one disputes that the human sex drive can overwhelm the rational mind as it cries out for satisfaction. But there is another cry that may accompany the sex drive, one that is more substantial if not as boisterous. This is the cry for intimacy. What then is the relationship between sexual desire and emotional intimacy?

Clark Gable, one of the preeminent movie stars of the 20th century, was once caught with a prostitute. He was asked, "Why would you, Clark Gable, who could have your choice of women, pay a woman for sex?" He said, "I don't pay a woman for sex. I pay a woman to go away after sex." What a striking example of sex without intimacy.

Intimacy, I dare say, is the precious pearl we all desire from our love relationships. The need for emotional intimacy is the substance behind the longing for love expressed in practically every romantic song or poem ever written. To be utterly known by another, and cherished for it, may be at the top of the list of things we desire beyond individual survival needs such as water, food and safety. Long after sexual desire passes, the need for intimacy persists. No one commits suicide over an absence of sex, but some do kill themselves over an absence of intimacy, which is loneliness.

Loneliness is abysmal, and yet intimacy is risky. Authentic emotional intimacy between two people involves an exchange of vulnerabilities, including the vulnerability to rejection. And rejection plucks the dreadful chords of abandonment and shame in most of us. This makes emotional nakedness far more perilous than mere bodily nakedness in sex.

This is a conundrum we all face regarding intimacy; live with loneliness or risk rejection. The ever-present sex drive is all too ready to step into that void to provide a soothing connection. But to surrender to sex while still emotionally defended further isolates the self that hungers for real intimacy. It may feel less risky to rely on fantasy, or one may seek to detach the emotions from sex. But then the sex act becomes little more than a pantomime of human closeness: sex without intimacy, pleasure without authentic meaning. That was how Clark Gable handled the dilemma.

So what's the problem with that? Are there not simple pleasures that are perfectly fine without attachment to meaning, such as feeling the sun on one's face? I would argue that all pleasures, even the sun on one's face, are enhanced by a connection to a greater significance and are diminished by the lack of connection. This is all the more true for far more complex pleasures such as sex, which influences one's concept of self on many levels.

Sexual pleasure unsustained by meaningful intimacy eventually drifts towards emptiness. The sex that once thrilled becomes ordinary, the pleasure thinner, failing to gratify in quite the same way as before. Nobody wants this, so the experience must then be artificially boosted to imitate depth and sustain excitement: more novel, more edgy, or more reliant on fantasy.

In contrast, the textures of meaningful pleasure are abundant, and become more accessible over time, not less accessible. We don't develop tolerance to meaningful pleasure; just the opposite. We savor meaningful pleasure with deepening sensitivity as time passes.

Consider the excitement of true love and devotion, where the mere touch of the beloved's hand may elicit long-lasting, passionate delight. The term "pleasurable" is inadequate to describe the contentment of sex nourished by unfettered emotional intimacy. This is a full and highly personalized experience.

Which brings us back to the use of pornography. Porn's essential feature is that it provides the user with a vivid experience of depersonalized sex, utterly bereft of intimacy, the thing we desire more dearly than sex. In porn viewing, nothing is demanded that would actually create intimate meaning between living human beings. Loneliness is temporarily soothed, rejection is avoided, but at a cost.

The viewer must see the sex actors, from the outset, as mere objects among many other objects that are used until their usefulness is used up. By emotionally attaching his sexual self to objects, the viewer objectifies not only the porn actors, but himself as well, so that a nonthreatening, fantasy version of intimacy can be held in the mind. And when the porn image that excites becomes banal, as it must, the viewer is progressively desensitized to sexual pleasure. Porn seems to yield benefits in the short term, but it is a losing strategy in the long term for pleasure-loving people.

Porn use is hostile to the examined life. It leaves one progressively dependent on untruth, the crutch of fantasy, and, over time, more lonely and less capable of emotional connection with a true intimate. Being insulated from our deepest emotions is living small, which increases the risk of anxiety, depression, and old-fashioned unhappiness. As an overall contributor to life satisfaction, porn is a thief disguised as a philanthropist.

The path that values emotional honesty and intimacy is

admittedly risky and requires persistent courage, but the rewards have to do with true love. Love is sublime, based on the truth, and very likely the best thing out there. Add the effects of alcohol consumption and sexual self-governance can be nonexistent. I've known many who were wounded by such situations.

# 13

# 444 and Counting

When I was a little boy, I learned numbers long before I could identify letters. I went around "reading" numbers and speaking them aloud wherever I saw them, probably driving my parents crazy, though they didn't let on. Counting was the closest thing I had to a superpower. Numbers also represented a connection to the wider world and access to something grand out there that preexisted me. Of course, I had no concrete grasp of that at the time. I just liked numbers.

One day I sat at the kitchen table and stayed there until I counted to one thousand, after which my patient mother rewarded me with a "Wowww! Very good, Jerry." In my memory it was a monumental achievement that took all day, though I now know it couldn't have taken longer than 30 minutes.

Another memorable experience with a number has yielded benefits to this very day. I was sitting alone on my bed with a large book, a dictionary I believe, reading the page numbers and searching for numbers hidden within the scribble-scrabble definitions. I came to page 444.

I said aloud to myself, "I'm four years old and this is my number: 444." And so it was. 444 was my number for life. Sure enough, since that day I've been inclined to speak aloud to myself the number 444 at random times. A year or longer may pass without my thinking of it and then, while standing on line at the bank or eating dinner with friends, up through the jumble of thought will rise, clear and bright, the number 444. Then in respectful solidarity with my younger self, I give soft utterance to my number: 444. My old friend 444 is fearless; it even came to my mind unbidden at the altar on my wedding day.

I never force myself to remember the number, never schedule an utterance, and I never fret that it will go away for good. Like the wind and the Holy Spirit, 444 comes and goes on its own mysterious timetable. The moment it appears and I acknowledge its presence is a pure moment for me, strangely stabilizing and free from anxiety. I always smile inwardly.

The mystery of 444 has not stopped me from attempting to assess its psychological or even spiritual significance. I easily reject the "primeval self" hypothesis, that this is a vestige of superstition. My relationship with the number has nothing in common with obsessive, compulsive behavior. I jokingly call 444 a superpower, but I do not call it a "higher power." I never pursue it and it doesn't have a necessary connection with agitation. 444 is a delightful curiosity that suggests to me how important a sense of continuity is in life.

The realization and the feeling that I am the same person as that little boy sitting on the edge of a bed with a dictionary imparts a welcome self-respect and compassion for myself; outlooks that I intuit are integral to my experience of a meaningful life.

Both sides of my family have researched our ancestral origins. Feeling connected to my dad's grandmother, who ran a farm in Poland in the 19th century, or sympathizing with the legal travails of a rascally great-grandfather in Italy stirs my soul in a way that's hard to define. I like being connected to them. What decisions did they make that affect my life today?

What decisions am I making today that will affect the lives of

others 100 years from now? I like being connected to them too. This is somewhat mind-blowing and pleasing to ponder.

I might extend this train of thought to wider society. The study of Western Civilization represents continuity with our cultural past, our intellectual and spiritual development as a race, and our connection with our younger selves as a civilization. You could say reading and rereading Plato's *Republic* or *Genesis* or Shakespeare's *King Lear* is a 444 of sorts for our culture; touchstones of continuous development, memory and meaning; each reader a present link between the past and the future.

I once worked at St. John's College in Annapolis, Maryland. One of its founders, the strangely named Stringfellow Barr, was a strong advocate of admitting talented students to the College before they graduated high school. He said, "The only thing you learn in the last two years of high school is how to dance!" This is not earth-shattering information, but I like that statement. It helped me feel closer to Stringfellow Barr. In its small way this brought greater meaning to my labor at the College.

Speaking out the seemingly trivial "444" whenever it calls to me allows me to feel closer to the boy I was. This makes it easier to accept myself as I am now, since that boy and I are one and the same human being. It is so odd and wonderful to me that life is like that; that a small, obscure moment over fifty years ago can transcend my present hardships and find lasting purchase in my soul.

# 14

# The True Explorer

It may seem trite to say life is a journey, but few metaphors are more apt for describing the human experience. Personal insight and awareness often have the same gradual, unfolding nature that mirrors the action of putting one foot in front of the other. Moment to moment we are keenly conscious about the desire to be somewhere else, to know what we don't know, or to acquire something still outside our grasp. Far from being trite, understanding life as a journey is quite meaningful and useful for facing life's difficulties. Humans respond to the call for a better life by moving from point A to point B, physically, mentally or spiritually.

The impulse to physically wander is inherited from our ancient vegetarian ancestors, and the need to settle down in a base, cave, den or tribal territory is characteristic of carnivores. So says the legendary explorer Bruce Chatwin in his intriguing collection of essays, *The Anatomy of Restlessness*. The omnivorous design of our teeth and the versatile structure of the human body hint at the acceptability of both lifestyles: roaming the land in search of sustenance or staying put in one place to construct agreeable ways to cook and eat. Even today for many, nothing says home like a great kitchen and dinner table.

So we have competing desires: the urge to travel, to move, to be curious, as well as the longing to nest and rest. The moment we answer the call to explore we've also sown seeds for the yearning for home.

There's beauty in that tension. To wander without a literal or figurative sense of home is to be lost, to be pushed without the stabilizing pull. The explorer may physically go in one direction, but psychologically he desires a round trip; to come back to his familiar self, but with something new added. There is a heroic departure from the norm and a return, hopefully with new gifts to offer, leading to a new and better normal.

Historically, Chatwin reports, the nomad doesn't wander aimlessly, but follows known paths of migration; the geographic familiarity perhaps compensating for the absence of a fixed address. You could say the nomad is uncivilized, if we accept Chatwin's definition of civilized as "living in cities." The true nomad or explorer is something of a disruptive influence on civil society. His path goes outside the boundaries, but his motives are constructive. His movement seeks provision or insight or economic gain, not escape.

Chatwin cites the Greek historian Herodotus, himself an exile and a traveler with boundless curiosity. In *The Histories Book IV* we find a fascinating description of the advantages of nomadic life. Facing military aggression by the Persian King Darius, the nomadic Scythians went on the move. But what appeared as retreat to Darius was nothing of the sort. The Scythians merely acted in accord with their accustomed lifestyle. In frustration, Darius sent a message to the Scythian King: "Why do you always run away? " The Scythian King replied, "I have never fled for fear of any man, nor do I now flee from you. If you really want a fight, find the graves of our fathers and then you'll see whether we'll fight. As for your boast that you are my master, go and cry." Soon enough Darius was the one retreating.

Nomadic traditions are highly spiritual; having gave rise to the great world religions. Abraham, Moses, Jesus, Buddha, Mohammed—all nomads. Chatwin, an agnostic, writes, "...no great transcendental faith has ever been born of an Age of Reason. Civilization is its own religion."

Chatwin proposes, however, that the estrangement of physical movement from spiritual growth in civilization contributes to a stagnation we seek to recapture in focused migrations. The Muslim Hajj and other pilgrimages endeavor to balance the loss of human movement inherent to civilization.

Chatwin came of age in the 1960s. In many ways he embodied a daring and progressive lifestyle that typified those times. But he was primarily a freethinking intellectual who didn't hesitate to call out the posers among his contemporaries.

Chatwin disdained the recreational drug use associated with that age, regarding it not as counter-cultural but as counterfeit and still bound by middle-class material values. This didn't endear him to "the cool kids" of his time. He saw his own generation as profoundly ignorant of the worth of travel and exploration as purposeful activities, ways to test one's imagination and develop skills, not as excuses for idleness and indulgence. But since humans must journey, it didn't surprise him that people were susceptible to seeking inferior journeys of the chemical kind.

Chatwin disrupted his society and spurred his own growth by moving his body. He believed walking was best because, taking his cue from nature, the best things in life are accomplished slowly and deliberately. Writing in 1970 he said, "All our activities are linked to the idea of journeys..., our brains have an information system giving us our orders for the road, and that here lie the mainsprings of our restlessness. At an early stage man found that he could spill out all this information in one go, by tampering with the chemistry of the brain. He could fly off on an illusory journey or an imaginary ascent..., but true wanderers rarely fell prey to this illusion. Drugs are for people who have forgotten how to walk."

The horizon of the inner journey is where Chatwin ultimately set his sights. His concept of adventure had little to do with adrenaline-pumping risks or gawking at the exotic, though he did take risks and he did witness the exotic. His concept of adventure involved responding to restlessness without surrender to rootlessness.

There was boldness and maybe even impulsivity to his adventures. He stepped outside of his known territory but not outside of his consciousness. His first and perhaps best-known book, *In Patagonia*, came about because of a conversation with an elderly friend. The friend said, "I'm too old to go to Patagonia now. Please go for me!"

Chatwin answered the call and left immediately, famously sending this succinct message of resignation to his employer: "Have gone to Patagonia."

If life is a journey, then to sojourn well, we must be in it for the long term and be willing to go beyond known territory. There will be long stretches where nothing seems to be happening. The true explorer is patient and makes peace with the step-by-step nature of the process. I admire the abandon with which Bruce Chatwin accepted those facts.

Think of the life of learning as a long walk. Better yet, take a long walk and explore. You get to know things better when they go by slowly.

# 15

# I Dig Your Mirth

In the late 1970s I lived in a rural university town where a significant number of people were thought of as hippies. They rejected prevailing bourgeois values and led back-to-the-land lifestyles. I respected their bold, independent ways and imagined myself a kindred spirit, even though I myself was thoroughly bourgeois.

One day I was reading a book in the "radical cafe" near the campus when a hippy-man sat down at my table. Sharing tables was common in that cafe, which espoused a more Marxist, communal way of doing things. When I glanced up from my book to acknowledge the man, he started talking. Eventually he explained his philosophy of life and his solutions for what ailed the human race. One of his big ideas involved bananas.

He said, "Everyone's so depressed and you know why?" I did not. "They don't have enough potassium, man! If everyone ate bananas, they'd get enough potassium and they wouldn't be depressed. It's all in the bananas!" This made me laugh and so we talked for a while, enjoying each other's company, laughing at each other's jokes. When he got up to leave, he paused and with genuine sweetness said, "I dig your mirth, man." We shook hands and then he was gone and I never saw him again. But the memory of him and our brief but warm encounter still makes me smile and appreciate the connecting power of humor.

Sometimes humor can penetrate our discouragement when all else has failed. Ten years ago a friend of mine was admitted to an inpatient addiction treatment clinic. I sat with him for moral support while a staff counselor conducted the orientation interview. For my friend, entering rehab was a moment of real defeat—just barely better than going to jail.

The counselor asked, "Do you smoke cigarettes?" My friend looked at her with despair, as if this were the final indignity, and answered, "I'm trying to quit" —which made all three of us laugh out loud, considering where we were. I greatly appreciated his sense of humor and how it slightly but significantly mitigated his misery in this situation. Mirth at its best is a shared experience that has power to reduce obstacles to intimacy. When I worked with incarcerated men, laughter was a great therapeutic tool that often eased them closer to each other, creating bonds and softening the hardened edges that men sometimes form around their deep sadness. As one inmate astutely observed, "If I didn't laugh, I'd cry, but laughing makes crying feel better."

A shared laugh is a great leveler, a way to feel human together, even a way to restore dignity. Raoul Wallenberg was a Swedish diplomat in Hungary during WWII who saved tens of thousands of Jews from extermination. After the war, he was arrested by his former Soviet allies and charged with espionage. It's presumed he was taken to Siberia, and was never heard from again.

Information about Wallenberg in captivity is scant, but one prisoner who escaped a brutal Soviet labor camp described a brief but humorous encounter with the great man. One day as Wallenberg was being treated roughly by his captors he called out, "Taxi!" —much to the amusement of his fellow prisoners who, despite their privations, were heartened by his gutsy gallows humor.

A sense of humor in the face of suffering can be a saving grace that strengthens resilience and suggests a spark of hope. When we laugh, we are fully present in the moment, if only briefly. The clarity of that present-ness is pleasing despite what other burdens we carry. As they say, laughter is good medicine, but it can also be good food, water, and oxygen.

While traveling in India, I lived for a time in a third-floor apartment adjacent to a beautiful park. I immediately learned that a Hindu worship group gathered in the park beneath my window every morning at 7AM. What a drag. I was hoping I could sleep late most mornings. Their meetings lasted one hour and always ended with *laughter yoga*.

Laughter yoga involves group members looking directly at each other and forcing laughter, in the belief that feigned laughter is as beneficial to the body and soul as spontaneous laughter. I noticed it didn't take long for the fake laughter to become genuine, leaving the whole group cracking up for real. Sometimes I'd stand at the window and tell jokes at my normal volume and pretend to enjoy the hysterics of my "audience." What might have been a noisy nuisance became a secretly shared mirth that helped me feel tenderness towards this group of devotees.

Mirth may be a higher order of humor, a deeper kind of delight. The poet William Blake said, "Too much fun is of all things most loathsome. Mirth is better than fun, and happiness is better than mirth." It is reasonable to me that a growing sense of mirth, rather than a growing cynicism, is a tremendous asset for a happy life. "Mirth is better than fun" is a strange sounding phrase to the modern ear, which distinguishes very little between the two.

Contemporary life offers countless options for mirthless fun, empty entertainment, and banal diversions. Mirth, on the other hand, is uplifting and informative; it has meaningful content. It brings people together and leaves a person physically and emotionally healthier when concluded.

Mirth is not sarcastic; it banishes the critical voice that brings toxic judgment to ourselves or to others. A mirthful approach to life may be akin to meditation, attending fully to the present moment, the opposite of escapism. I wonder how much sooner we'd hear whispers of contentment in our souls if we intentionally cultivated a humorous or mirthful filter for the moments of our day that might otherwise be irritating or discouraging. Mirth enlarges our capacity to take on the poignant struggles of life.

For these reasons and others, I dig mirth, too. And with all due respect to my long-lost hippy friend, I'd say mirth is probably better than bananas.

# 16

# Endings and Beginnings

As a kid, after my parents put me and my sisters to bed, I would sometimes sneak back out to a hidden spot on the stairwell to eavesdrop on the adult conversation. My mother and father seemed happier at that time of night, and I was soothed by their relaxed voices and unguarded laughter. I suspect I also hungered for a secret connection with them and for reassurance that the grown-up world was well in control of everything good in life.

Around that time President John F. Kennedy was assassinated. I was five years old. My strongest memory of that event was how upset the grown-ups were, and how uncensored were their distraught reactions in front of me as the news spread. I had no anxiety about the reality of death, unaware as I was at that age of endings and beginnings, so this window into the adult realm was exciting. It felt as if I were eavesdropping on the whole grown-up world.

A few weeks after that, an old man who lived on our street also died. This was my first encounter with the death of someone personally known to me and it did upset me. When someone dies it means they go away, I realized. I became concerned about the most important old person in my life, my grandmother.

"Mom, is grandma going to die?" I asked.

"Oh, don't say that!" she said, wincing. And so we didn't talk about death. But I sure wanted to talk about it, and I did with an older boy on my street. He let me in on the shocking, if open, secret: "Everybody dies someday," he said. "Even you."

His words hit hard. If I was going to die someday, then where would I go? The grownups' severe reactions to the President getting shot now had a different feeling to it. Everybody dies someday. If the grown-ups were not in control of this then who was? I recall a sharp increase of anxiety in my life at that time. Dying wasn't just for old people, and I was certain I didn't want to die.

By nature, everything in us fights to live, and yet that's ultimately a losing battle. The billions of human lives currently on Earth will nearly all be gone in another century, replaced by others who will also die. The suggestion of meaninglessness and possible annihilation could easily tempt one to cynicism, despair, or worse. Joseph Conrad captures the sickening emptiness in the bald apprehension of death through his narrator in *Heart of Darkness*:

*I have wrestled with death. It is the most unexciting contest you can imagine. It takes place in an impalpable greyness, with nothing underfoot, with nothing around, without spectators, without clamour, without glory, without the great desire of victory, without the great fear of defeat, in a sickly atmosphere of tepid skepticism, without much belief in your own right, and still less in that of your adversary.*

No wonder my own sweet mother found death difficult to talk about. But we must talk about it and face the anxiety that may attend it. As psychologist Irvin Yalom writes, "...given the centrality of death in our existence, given that life and death are interdependent, how can we possibly ignore it?" Well, we can't truly ignore the terror of death for long, nor should we. "Though the physicality of death destroys us," Yalom continues, "the idea of death may save us." An intriguing paradox for sure, but how do we make sense of it in the present?

We find help in an essay entitled *Ignorance*, by philosopher Wendell Berry, where he expounds on how a human being, properly subordinated to the limits of his human nature and life, may experience, not terror, but simultaneous grief and joy, where death and life embrace as collaborators, not adversaries.

To illustrate, Berry describes one of the fascinating subplots of *King Lear* where the Earl of Gloucester, once a politically powerful man now blinded, destitute and suicidal, is aided by Edgar, the son he falsely accused and drove away. Edgar conceals his identity in order to help his blind father.

In an intense father-son role reversal, Edgar becomes his father's physical and spiritual guide, leading the despondent Gloucester into thinking he's thrown himself off a cliff to die, when in reality the Earl leaps off only a small rise of ground, high enough to be jarring but not fatal. Edgar, the consummate benevolent trickster, pretends further to be a passerby who, after witnessing the failed suicide attempt, proclaims these transformative words to the still despairing Gloucester:

*Thy life's a miracle. Speak yet again.*

Edgar's life-affirming, grown-up words eventually call Gloucester back from the childlike despair and anxiety that led him to give up on his humanity, Berry observes. When Gloucester was able to look past the earthly reality of life and death to embrace the miraculous, rooted in the sublime mystery of human existence, his humanity was restored and his life preserved. Somewhere between the fearful child-self and the grandiose god-self was the actual man, whose life was worth living.

Gloucester was guilty of the hubris of the powerful that thinks human life may be agreeably and reliably manipulated if one is powerful enough or shrewd enough. In his arrogance, Gloucester "treated life as knowable, predictable and in his control," writes Berry. This mechanistic view denies the miraculous and the mysterious, and regards life as a commodity subject to man, rather than man being subject to life and its constraints. As they say in the 12-Step recovery world, unless we accept life on life's terms, we are headed for misery.

Misery came to Gloucester in his crushing fall from power, leading him to give up on his human life and choose death, though suicide is not the only way to give up on one's humanity, Berry contends.

Gloucester gave up on his humanity long before his political defeat; his desire to die was merely a further representation of his hubris. "Gloucester's attempted suicide is really an attempt to recover [god-like] control over his life – a control he believes (mistakenly) he once had and lost. The nature of his despair is delineated in his belief that he can control his life by killing himself," writes Berry.

A modern-day version of that hubris may be the common belief that with enough time, talent and money one can get everything one wants in life. But the obvious reality is that man did not birth himself and making himself a god cannot prevent loss and grief and death. With one foot in life and the other in death, the warped and fallen god-man Kurtz in *Heart of Darkness* urges us to avoid his fate; his warning offered in his death whispers: "The horror! The horror!"

According to Wendell Berry, and perhaps William Shakespeare, grasping that "life is a miracle" involves releasing one's ultimate trust in human agency—the desperate pursuit of a life without limits—which is an anxiety-ridden quest for the un-miraculous.

Gloucester eventually takes heed to this warning and has a different end than Kurtz. He recognizes, for possibly the first time, the truth of his limits, his endings, which yields a strang and peaceful joy out of his grief — a new beginning. He reclaims his life, and his inspired utterance is almost a psalm:

> *You ever-gentle gods, take my breath from me;*
> *Let not my worser spirit tempt me again*
> *To die before you please.*

Twenty years after JFK's death, at a time I felt great anxiety about the grown-up world I was now supposed to inhabit, I was at my precious grandmother's bedside in the hospital. She was unconscious, and dying. I was trying to talk to her, hoping she could hear me. One of my uncles arrived and stood at the foot of the bed and began to cry, which provoked others present to cry as well.

Upset and frightened as I was, I might have cried too, but I didn't. Instead, a mysterious awareness settled on me, a peaceful and ecstatic touch, that made all other concerns pale. I suddenly had a strong sense, even a knowledge, that my grandmother was going to be alright in death, and that I was going to be alright in life. It was the utmost opposite of anxiety, a simultaneous ending and beginning, and it was awesome.

As I witnessed the end of a life I loved — my grandmother's — Life itself seemed far more expansive and grander than I imagined before. There was nothing I needed to make different or control. Life just was, and it was good. In that miraculous moment I was enabled to better accept Life on its own terms, how it begins and ends, to be okay with my existence in it, and also be okay with the "ever-gentle gods" who will decide my death, when it pleases them.

# 17

# The Need to Read

For book lovers, being stuck in a place without something good to read can be a painful affair. I found myself in that position recently in the remote, small town of Buncrana, Ireland. I finished the books I had on hand and had no success finding anything interesting in the disorganized book bins of the "Charity Shops" on Main Street.

A kind soul told me there was a funky used bookstore in Letterkenny, a larger nearby town. Fortune smiled on me because just then a bus going to Letterkenny rumbled down the street. I flagged it down and off I went. A car would cut the travel time in half, but lacking a vehicle I resigned myself to enduring forty-five vacant minutes on the bus without anything to read.

Once on-board though, my attention was piqued by the other passengers. There was a young couple in lively conversation. The woman's speech was clear enough, but the man's rapid and thick Irish brogue was as indecipherable to me as Swahili. It was fun trying to speculate on what he said by what she said.

We passed a bus going in the opposite direction. Our taciturn driver and theirs exchanged a polite wave. How do I know it was a polite wave and not the wave of old friends, or of rivals, or of brothers? Well, I don't. I wondered what the two men's stories were.

An elderly man sat a little ahead of me across the aisle, silent and motionless. Suddenly he lifted his head in time to see a small stone church with a graveyard pass by. Communing with a grace known only to him, he gently crossed himself before resuming his silent meditation.

This led me to direct my attention to my own inner world. Why was I even on this bus? Oh yes, book hunting, but why? It's fun, but what was I really after? The joy of reading and learning? The avoidance of boredom? Maybe, but there was something else. As I thought about my need to read, a fifty-year-old memory startled me.

When my older sister first went off to kindergarten, I was bereft. To console me my mother took me on walks through the neighborhood, saying, "Let's see if we can find something important!" This was great fun for me, even though I didn't know what *important* meant. My little world came alive with the thrill of the hunt as I focused my attention on items I usually ignored. There was a bottle cap. "Mom, is this important?" It was important to my sister, who used bottle caps for her artwork. Into my pocket it went. There's a stick, twisted in a weird way. How about a soda can? Finding a penny was like gold.

Pondering this memory while on a bus rolling through the Irish countryside, I entered into an extraordinary feeling of connection with my mom and with my curious younger self. Surely in my present book hunt I was reenacting something, likewise hoping to "find something important." I felt full and rich as I sat with these feelings linking past and present; a small but pleasing insight into my current behavior.

Whatever mental state this was—excitement, contentment, love—I was in a good place. This bus ride was anything but vacant. The thrill of paying attention to my present environment coincided with the joy of discovery; the delight of finding meaning and value where I previously thought there was none.

The gentle sweetness of this recollection reminded me to regard my attention as a precious thing, and to be more selective about where I placed it and not to squander it. This can be quite a challenge in a world that presents so many options for what to look at, listen to, and think about. It is far easier to passively respond to whatever presents itself the loudest or most urgent. This passivity can foster a sort of "learned helplessness" leading to a dependency on the loud and urgent for motivation.

A common example: a man is unable to complete an assignment until the deadline looms, thus manufacturing an urgency without which he can't command his energies and focus his attention to complete the task. The man insists he "needs" the tyrannizing last-minute pressure, because without it he believes nothing is happening within himself to draw from.

There are times in my day I am tempted to think nothing is happening, like when riding a bus or being in between this or that activity. This practice of directing my attention to the present moment, what is going on around me and within me right now, has proved to me that in the spaciousness of the human body and soul there is never nothing happening.

Practicing this attentiveness, sometimes called mindfulness, requires effort. But what a thrill when our powers of attention grow strong and nimble and can be employed freely. Perhaps the common usage of the term "will power" is better understood as attention power. This is a high order of freedom when achieved through natural effort. Yet the process can seem puzzling: I am doing something intentional, but I'm not fully in charge of the outcome. It is not the same as fantasizing or daydreaming as there is more discovery than creation going on, more surrender than orchestration.

This cultivated inner space has become a mental and emotional sanctuary for me; partly a place of refuge and also a place to do active work, seeing what's there and trying to understand it. It is a safe place where I can "find something important" among things previously ignored as insignificant or too unpleasant.

There I discover a need of mine that goes well beyond my immediate desires: the need to read the self. This kind of sanctuary is sometimes bittersweet, but even then, it is a lovely and meaningful place to be. And, I believe, it is within the reach of every person.

little hell in himself, while publicly pretending it did not exist – and when he was caught up in it, he was completely helpless."

Feeling helpless and vulnerable is dreadful, and we may do anything to avoid it, and so we tend to push down our deepest pain. But emotional pain doesn't always do as it is told; in fact, it never does for long. Though confined, it eventually surfaces anyway, but often disguised as depression, anxiety, shame, self-doubt, or even physical illness. Hidden wounds don't want to remain hidden. Still, a man hiding his sorrow is as old as the human race.

In his book *The Examined Life*, Stephen Grosz describes how we may feel trapped by our wounds, imprisoned by our own hidden history and react to it by repeating mistakes and self-defeating behaviors. Yet those same mistakes and self-defeating behaviors are also emissaries, delivering messages about something inside needing attention.

Grosz describes the experience of American soldiers captured during the Vietnam War. The soldiers, often kept in brutal solitary confinement, learned to communicate with each other through an ingenious system of tapping a code on the walls of the cells that separated them. Their tapping and listening skills became so sophisticated that they were able to discern, through only a few taps, the mood of the message sender; if he was hopeful or depressed, for example.

Marie Grosz quotes philosopher Simone Weil on this same phenomenon of prisoner tapping: "The wall is the thing which separates them but it is also their means of communication," she said. "Every separation is a link."

Walling off our emotional wounds to protect ourselves from further suffering is an understandable impulse. But the pain imprisoned inside us is tapping on the wall, always tapping, trying to forge a link to the conscious mind, to be understood, to be accepted, to be healed. Weil says the wall, "...is the barrier. At the same time, it is the way through." What beautiful irony that is; fortunate for us because it suggests the possibility our suffering, while often hideous, may contain the seeds of its own redemption. Our agonies and traumas are not meaningless; they can serve a greater good.

May I suggest one of those greater goods? One of the grotesque things about emotional woundedness is its cozy relationship with shame. The wound is bad enough by itself, but then we, the wounded, heap additional shame upon the wound. The shame is the jailer, keeping the wound locked up in darkness and secrecy, where it remains infected and able to exert its serpentine influence. Quite often the biggest difficulty to addressing the deep wound is getting past the shame that blocks access.

Entrenched shame does more than perpetuate misery from the wound, however. Shame is also an enemy to intimacy in relationships. And now we get to the heart of the matter. Here is the sensational greater good that emerges from the courageous work of facing old wounds.

By sharing our pain with a worthy other, someone who can listen with affection and not judgement, we begin learning how to become known, to be seen as we are: first to another, then to ourselves. We begin to experience the nourishing relationship between self-acceptance and intimacy, which is essential for the art of giving and receiving love with the whole self.

Beyond wounds, beyond grievances, beyond acclaim, beyond professional and material success, even beyond great sex, meaningful love reigns supreme. Love, based on the truth of who we are, is the pearl of great price.

Who would have thought that the dreaded experience of woundedness could be connected to the much-desired attainment of love? In the pilgrimage of life everything is connected, even as we attempt to disconnect things. You can see how holding onto old pain could be an effective defense against the risks of true intimacy.

But it's not really effective because we hear the tapping. As my lawyer friend discovered on his day of celebration, his greatest sorrow showed up as well; an uninvited guest, but one that would not be denied admittance.

Every separation is a link, is a terrifying and wonderful

statement. Intentionally seeking out our hidden pain may seem impossibly frightening at first, but if we incline our ears to the tapping and move towards the wall, we may end up getting what our wounded souls are really looking for.

# 19

# The Scream

Assuming one understands the language, listening to local radio programs is a great way for travelers to get a feel for the culture of a new place. While visiting Ireland I fell in love with all sorts of radio programs: news, interviews, music, and sports broadcasts. Journalists seemed unselfconscious and sincere, no matter the topic. The passionate, melodious Irish voice made even the Farm Report interesting.

Interviews with professional athletes in the United States are a cliché-ridden waste of time. But interviews with Irish athletes were great fun, with their quirky, honest comments such as explaining how a player was absent because he was still "on the piss," or the how certain referees were "wankers." There were personalities with great names like Mossy Quinn being asked, "So, can the Dubliners hold on to the lead, Mossy?" I loved hearing all their opinions. One sports commentator insisted that Muhammad Ali was Irish.

I recall my bafflement listening to a story about the

history of whoring. It was about how in the past only men were allowed to participate in whoring. In fact, whoring was just for men, period. If women tried to get involved with whoring, they were beaten and imprisoned.

How could that be? It took me a while, but I finally figured out the announcer was saying hurling, not whoring. Hurling is a beloved sport in Ireland, similar to field hockey. That made the story only slightly less weird.

From the radio talk shows I learned the Irish people were generous and open about receiving Syrian refugees. Also, the music programs were consistently interesting, assuming one didn't mind half of them being about Van Morrison. I happen to like his music, and so one day an advertisement for a band that played only Van Morrison music caught my eye. The band's unique approach was that all songs were to be sung, not in English, but in Irish.

This was intriguing, but I still hesitated because over the years I'd grown weary of live music shows. I frequently felt an awkward, self-conscious irritation with musicians for excessive "performing" — the contrived mugging and bizarre facial contortions they seem to think is required. "Just play the music!" I want to say. I usually prefer hearing music in a disembodied way; melodies wafting through the ether in the dark, sort of like one gets from the radio. I did buy a ticket for the concert though.

At the theatre it was general admission, so I snagged a front row seat. The crowd was middle-aged and mellow. Suddenly ten musicians pounced on to the stage and started rocking out, catching the audience off-guard.

This was good. There was something about this band that was straightforward and free of the performer's guile that usually bothered me. I knew many of the songs with the English lyrics, but there were several songs I'd never heard before. The Irish words were mesmerizing.

For a change I felt very unselfconscious, which mirrored my perception that the musicians were sincerely into each song, and not just "performing" in an affected way. I got into the songs too and was so enthused, I ceased paying attention to the crowd around me. It was just the band and me, jumping up, whooping it up, whatever I felt. The musicians on my side of the stage seemed to notice my antics and I think they liked it, smiling at me and nodding.

One of the songs I'd never heard before was *Ballerina*. That title suggests something pretty and delicate, but they played the song with a hard edge.

At one point the lead singer let loose a soulful howl, more like a scream. My eyes were locked on him and when he screamed, not only did he really mean it, but I felt like I was screaming as well, somehow inhabiting his scream, strange as that may sound. I'd never had that feeling before; it was connecting and transcending as if I had received the music into my body. My chest felt full of the emotion; the scream located dead center. In that moment an astonishing new thought exploded in my head: *I don't ever want to be ashamed of myself again!*

What in the world was that, I wondered, feeling stunned and relieved and delighted all at once. After the last song, the band ran off, but I clamored for an encore. When they came back out, the musicians near me also looked delighted; laughing and giving me a thumbs up.

I left the theatre feeling so light and airy, like I could fly home, but I just couldn't go home yet. I sat down on some steps and examined my surroundings. This was Main Street Letterkenny. The Autumn air was chill, I could smell pizza nearby and bought a slice. I saw lively people all around. I could hear a guitar player strumming somewhere; it was Saturday night. The eyes of my soul seemed to be directed outward in all directions, even as my senses took everything in. Unhindered by self-concern, I was accepting of everything I saw and felt, without judgment. The people seemed worthy of the highest love.

This was a state of super-receptivity, birthed by the music and the musicians, and consecrated by a scream. Yes, birthed and consecrated, but how was it conceived? I don't recall ever having screamed in my entire life. But this vicarious scream, from a song I didn't know in a language I couldn't understand, overshadowed my usual way of thinking things out. This was not something I did to myself; it was something received, like a radio transmission.

Again, I looked with affection at the people streaming this way and that, enjoying their proximity to me, feeling strangely close to them. And all the time I'm thinking: Wouldn't it be great if it were like this all the time?

# 20

# Beast-Angels Among Us

"I'll never forgive myself," Mary said pitifully. I was in an addiction treatment group circle with Mary and a dozen others. Twenty years before she had a baby girl who died. Though no charges were filed, Mary implied her drinking was a key factor in the circumstances that led to the baby's death. Now in her late forties, she was struggling to face this and other failures and humiliations caused by three decades of hard drinking.

Of all Mary's heartaches, the baby's death certainly seemed the most punishing. Our society reserves a special shaming for women judged as "bad mothers" — especially those who abuse substances. By declaring herself unforgivable, Mary gave voice to a shame heaped upon her by others and now she heaped it upon herself. Was she unforgivable as she supposed? The normally talkative group fell silent.

Finally, another woman spoke up and with great tenderness asked, "Mary, are there any advantages to not forgiving yourself?"

"No, there's nothing good about not forgiving yourself," she answered.

"Then why do you continue to not forgive yourself?"

"I don't know," said Mary.

The questioner persisted, but not unkindly, "I think maybe there is something you find useful about not forgiving yourself. Can you think of what that might be?"

"No." There was now an edge of defiance in Mary's voice.

"As long as you don't forgive yourself for your baby's death," the woman said softly, "you have a reason to continue drinking."

Now this was a twist I didn't expect. The intensity of the insight gave me goosebumps.

By the time the group was over Mary seemed relieved, her burdensome secret somewhat lifted. Why then did she collude with her miserable shame for so many years by declaring herself incapable or unwilling to forgive herself? The answer is that she was in truth colluding with her addiction, of which paralyzing shame was a terrible symptom.

As they say, addiction is the human condition writ large, and the shame dynamic we observe in Mary's life is likely universal to the human condition. As Ernest Kurtz writes in his outstanding book *Shame and Guilt*:

*Shame contains a "not" – the "not" imposed by essential limitation. That "not" is to be neither severed nor undone: it is lodged in the very essence of our human be-ing. To be honestly human is to be aware that one falls short – to accept that the ability to be is also the ability to be not. Thus, to be human is to experience shame – to feel "bad" about the not-ness lodged in one's essence.*

To say human beings feel "bad" about shame is a vast understatement. Shame is agonizing and fear of exposure leads us to expend enormous mental and emotional energy to keep shame well hidden, even defending its foul existence with declarations like, "I will never forgive myself" or "I will always feel this way." When shame is exerting its power, we hide — and human connection is lost. Shame brings isolation, alienation, and loneliness. One cannot begin to measure the sum of human misery in the world attributable to this.

Why does shame feel bad? Does it have to? Kurtz observes the painful power of shame stems from how deeply rooted is our conflicted response to our dual nature as beast-angels.

Why this feeling-bad of shame? Because of the anomalous nature of the human as beast-angel, as essentially limited yet craving unlimitedness. The anomaly is inherent, for to be human is to be "both/and" rather than "either/or." Confronted with the task of being human, one must live both its polarities: one cannot be only either... Inevitably one falls short of being either beast or angel – neither can be total so long as both are actual.

Beast-angels: rational-animals. The "angel" represented by all that is uniquely human: our reason, the ability to think conceptually, to aspire for the eternal, to live principled lives, examined lives, and maybe even to love. The "beast" in us is represented by the body and all that is demanding and finite about it. Despite its wondrous beauty it is also crude, it harasses us with its desires and attachments, and it will weaken and die someday.

In *The Denial of Death*, Ernest Becker bluntly states human beings are "gods who shit" and that we are typically burdened and shamed by the contrast. It's not hard to observe people who attempt to resolve this by alternately living all one way or the other:  do the "responsible" thing during the week, party hard on weekends. This is a distraction from the more difficult work of reconciling the two natures.

The process of resolving the shame-filled dread of one's life begins with self-acceptance. Self-acceptance means accepting one's human limitations. This cannot be done in secret, it requires renewing open connections, reversing the isolation with supportive and understanding human beings, the way Mary did it in the group. As Kurtz puts it, "…to be real is to be limited, and to be limited is to be real, for limitation proves reality." This understanding enables joyous acceptance of the human condition.

For beast-angels like us, self-acceptance bridges the gap between the two natures, reducing shame and making self-forgiveness possible. When we are okay with all "we be" and all "we be not" the fruit is sublime, spontaneous, unavoidable joy. People often speak of this experience of shame being lifted as an awakening.

The strange and wonderful paradox is this: In self-acceptance we are most open to genuine change. In self-condemnation we consent to remain the same. I often hear people talk of "finding themselves" as if the process is nothing but one happy discovery after another. But facing ourselves as beast-angels means embracing the light and the shadow co-existing within. As Ernest Kurtz writes: "… accepting the reality of self-as-feared is the essential pre-condition of finding the reality of self-as-is."

# 21

# Spiritual but Not Religious

An atheist friend once caught me off-guard when she declared, "There's a reason for everything." It turns out she meant there is a rational, scientific explanation for everything that exists or happens, not that there is a Divine Purpose behind events. Her faith is in scientific progress to bring safety and stability to her life and to reveal life's mysteries, given enough time. Despite this apparent secular worldview, she calls herself spiritual.

As for so many, her spirituality focuses on personal growth and her desire to be in sync with natural forces governing the known world and holding it together. This spirituality also favors ethical, psychological, and political interests more than metaphysical ones. There is no necessary belief in the existence of a spirit realm or souls that live on after the body dies, much less faith in a religious concept of God.

This disenchantment with traditional ideas of God and long-established creeds has led to popular use of the phrase *spiritual but not religious* (SBNR). The implication is that individualized beliefs are more consciously arrived at and are more sophisticated and equipped to handle the complexities of modern life. World religions based on the embrace of objective truth are assumed obsolete — too rigid and narrow to serve the needs of individuals in the Information Age.

Acclaimed film director Martin Scorsese lamented the difficulty getting top actors interested in his religious-themed movie *Silence*, saying, "Several actors didn't want to get involved with anything that smacks of religion in any way." It's curious that those calling themselves religious are usually comfortable calling themselves spiritual, but the point of SBNR is to maintain a clear distinction from religion.

The phrase *spiritual but not religious* was popularized by Bill Wilson, one of the founders of Alcoholics Anonymous. He believed the desire for intoxication was primarily a spiritual impulse and that alcoholics were unconsciously trying to "grope their way to God" as they sought reliable fulfillment in alcohol.

In Bill Wilson's view, religious belief requires a higher order of maturity and complexity than does mere spirituality. But even as he greatly respected religion, Wilson made clear that Alcoholics Anonymous did not require religiosity for recovery from addiction. His use of SBNR was a practical and wise acknowledgement of legitimate emotional wounds some alcoholics suffered in their religious upbringing. A large number of alcoholics also had an aversion to anything churchy, stemming from religions' typically moralistic approach to alcoholism. For him SBNR was a frank statement of humility, the need for rudimentary spiritual assistance, and was not necessarily a declaration of permanent independence from religion. Wilson insisted, "...good theology ought to ask every man's question: Do I live in a rational universe under a just and loving God, or do I not?" His AA sought to provide emotional room for alcoholics to get physically well while still wrestling with that question.

Wilson and his co-founder Bob Smith chose the term higher power, not highest power or God, to assist alcoholics in their efforts. Wilson and Smith might have found it ironic and maybe disheartening to see the modern practice of the SBNR idea move away from religious thought, rather than towards it.

Still, many calling themselves SBNR do believe in a non-material realm and even cite experiential "touches" of the transcendent without specific mention of God. This person finds in a spiritual practice a bridge to the mysterious, and a way to gain agency over fearful and potentially threatening things in the experience of living. Love is often identified as the ultimate spiritual value, having mystical and protective properties within itself without a necessary connection to deity. *God is love* evolves into *Love is God*, with fear being the primary antagonist to spiritual growth.

Oprah Winfrey espouses this approach in her faith declaration, "I believe every single event in life happens [as] an opportunity to choose love over fear." The objective is a therapeutic one, based on a personal growth model of spirituality rather than on obedience to the will and purposes of one God, or gods, or a higher power. The road map to love means first loving the self: one must listen to oneself and follow one's own dreams.

This approach may even lead to organized groups and communal rituals, but without a defined object of worship that is higher than the self, the desire for self-fulfillment becomes the foremost concern and the primary power with which to contend. One's intentions are imbued with a quasi-omnipotence, attaining divinity status. If one's intentions are faithfully released to the larger Universe, then the divine in oneself aligns with the divine in the Universe to bring the intentions to fulfillment, goes the belief.

American political discourse increasingly appropriates this self-help language to stigmatize opposing views as necessarily fear-based. Political opinions and actions are less frequently assessed in a moral context as right and wrong, or even in a utilitarian way as better or worse, but instead as choices between one view or a fear of that view. A SBNR might dismiss an opposing point-of-view as a symptom of mental instability or as an irrational fear: something-phobic.

Despite the potential inaccuracy of that linguistic ploy, it may well be that the reaction against fear, or more specifically anxiety, is common ground for both the self-described SBNR and the religious person. Every human being has a keen desire to be free from internal anxiety. This is not a new concept emerging from the uncertainties of modern life. How to understand anxiety within the human condition reflects ancient questions and conundrums between philosophy and theology.

Do we reason our way to transcendence or are we awakened to it, as something revealed? Is spirituality generated from within or received from on high? Are human beings like onions whose crusty, brittle exterior just needs to be peeled off to reach the pure center? Or are we tainted throughout and in need of transformation? Every side to these questions has had its true believers for thousands of years.

How then does the modern seeker find clarity with such long-standing questions that have challenged the greatest minds of all time? I'm exceedingly reluctant to say what others should do, but here is an account of a spiritual experience that gave me some clarity I desperately needed, illuminated beyond intellect.

At age 21 I decided to give college life another try. My previous attempt was interesting but directionless, so I quit and went to work. After several low-paying jobs serving affluent people, I was resentful and became determined to not be among those who bowed to the rich. Back at a different university, I was hungry for knowledge and ambitious to learn something useful.

Despite my enthusiasm I was very nervous about my future. But living with chronic anxiety was so normal for me that I wasn't aware life could be conducted any other way. At the time I described myself as spiritual but not religious, though I understood very little of what I meant by that. In the midst of my confusion I had the first truly spiritual experience I am aware of, which happened shortly after my arrival on campus.

It was a Saturday afternoon and I was lounging around my dorm room when there was a loud knock on the door, a guy from down the hall. "Hey JJ, you wanna make twenty-five bucks for two hours work?" You better believe I did. This was 1979 when minimum wage was three dollars an hour, so this was good money. Off I went with him. "What are we going to do?" I asked. "Sell t-shirts," he said.

A famous rock band was playing at the big arena on campus and there were already long lines of people outside waiting to get in. I was introduced to the boss-man and he explained the deal: we were to sell bootleg t-shirts outside the arena.

The official and legal merchandise happened inside the arena and were totally controlled by the band. We were illegal so keep your head down, he said, and if you see the campus police, keep moving. T-shirts were $5.00 each and I was given a box of them filled to the brim.

The boss let us in on an innovative sales technique: since we would run out of XL sized t-shirts first, we could still sell a t-shirt to someone requesting XL by reaching into the box with both hands, one hand holding a shirt and the other holding the tag that had the size labeled on it. Then, he instructed us, quickly pull out the t-shirt with one hand, thus ripping off the tag in the process. This way the buyer couldn't see they were getting a medium or large-sized t-shirt instead of the XL they requested.

You might think cheating the customer this way would arouse pangs of conscience. But at that time, despite my claim to a personal spirituality, I placed greater value on personal shrewdness. I was determined to never play the fool for anyone. I found satisfaction in ripping off institutions and groups of people, especially if I considered the groups to be wealthy. It was vanity and avarice that really governed my thinking, but I easily deluded myself into believing I was striking a blow for the common man. I was a big fan of *Steal This Book* by Abbie Hoffman, the Yippie leader, who advocated small acts of subversive criminality to undermine the established order.

On the surface I affected a confident pose about myself, but deep inside I felt the confusion of my sloppy value system. In a conversation with a "religious" guy a week before I had asked, quite sincerely, "How do you know the difference between right and wrong?" He said, "When I'm considering the morality of an action, I ask myself two questions: Does this please God, and does this glorify God?" I had no idea what he meant by glorify God. It sounded like the kind of high-handed religious talk I was moving away from. Pleasing God seemed simple enough though, in theory. Just do good deeds.

Back at the arena I began walking around with my box of t-shirts. They sold quickly, with people gathering around thrusting five-dollar bills at me. In twenty minutes I had sold several dozen and I had a fistful of cash to show for it. I was feeling flush with success, but then I reached the point where someone asked for an XL t-shirt and I had no more of them. As instructed, I accomplished the maneuver of slyly removing the tag, thus cheating the customer.

As I mentioned, this normally wouldn't have bothered me much. I would have fairly easily convinced myself that the larger objective of getting over on a big corporation, even a rock and roll one, justified this smaller indiscretion against the customer. But for some reason those arguments weren't available to me this time. My stomach felt queasy.

I stepped aside to sort out my thoughts. The two questions I'd heard the week earlier came unbidden to my mind: Was this pleasing to God? Was this glorifying to God? My stomach still hurt.

No, it wasn't, I decided. What I was doing was neither pleasing to God nor glorifying to God—how could it be? I immediately found the boss and gave him all the money and remaining t-shirts and told him I quit and didn't want any payment. "What's wrong?" he asked, holding the wad of cash. I surprised myself by saying, "It's not honest," the words coming out all by themselves. He smirked and said, "You'll learn someday."

As I walked back to the dorm a startling euphoria settled on me. At the same time, I felt lifted up, like I was walking on air, relieved and happy.

Back in my room I put on a record, a Beethoven

symphony. The music rose and I could almost see it filling the tiny room and swirling about. I was possessed by a beautiful sweetness, completely free from anxiety, at least for now. This moment was clear, utterly sober, and superior to any experience I had before. Something far more expansive than myself was present and drawing me closer.

I mark that day as my first conscious contact with a spiritual…something. Or was it religious? This much I understood: it was something new I lacked within myself by nature, something far grander than I could then fathom, and something that changed the way I felt about living. It was exciting, like finding a treasure or falling in love. I wanted to pursue it.

I pondered my religious friend's advice. Pleasing God was about choosing right over wrong, I reasoned. But my understanding of right over wrong was incomplete, I intuited, until I could understand the second question. What was it to glorify God?

The following summer some help came my way. I was leisurely strolling in downtown Manhattan on a beautiful sunny day, feeling great. A man sidled up next to me, matching my pace. It was a workman carrying a large package on his shoulder.

"How's your faith?" he asked.

A little surprised, I said, "Good, I guess."

He had the word *Shekinah* emblazoned on his t-shirt.

"What's Shekinah?" I asked.

He said, "God's glory."

"Really?" There it was again. "But what is it?"

"Shekinah is the manifestation of God's presence on Earth. With you, maybe. See ya."

He turned sharply into a building and was gone.

A shiver of recognition passed through me, thinking of my uplifting experience of months before. Could that euphoria be a Shekinah? What an interesting thought this was. I no longer cared if this new glow I had since then was called spiritual or religious or even weird — it was just too splendid to worry about that.

The workman used the word presence — yes, it was that. A veil I didn't know existed was lifted, certainly not by my powers of reason or imagination. A highly personal presence that was not mine had beckoned me in. It was sublime, and yes, glorious, I concluded. If this was God's glory on Earth, I was more than willing to call it Shekinah and follow where it led me.

Whatever Shekinah was, it banished my anxiety. I wondered what more I could do to glorify God. Maybe all I needed to do was stay out of the way and Shekinah would come to me as before.

In the end I settled on calling this a spiritual experience. It changed me and set me on the spiritual path I'm on to this day. A path that draws me along — I take steps without knowing exactly where the path will lead. But as I take them my natural anxiety is muted and I am aware of a growing assurance that however my future unfolds, I am going to be okay.

# ACKNOWLEDGEMENTS

A special thank you goes to Jan Best de Vries of the Nanny Maria Wilhelmina de Vries Foundation in Baarn, the Netherlands, the first publisher of this collection.

I am deeply grateful for the community of readers, writers, editors, and thinkers who have offered their generous assistance on our common paths of personal growth: Tommy Bonn, Su3san Borden, Eva Brann, Jerry Bunker, Josh Burleigh, Nancy Calabrese, Doug Calhoun, Ben Clough, Kirstie Dodd, Cinar Doruk, Mark Doyon, Mark Dubis, Robert Eringer, Susan Everett, Larry Fischer, Erin Fitzpatrick, Michael W. Fogleman, Monica Galligan, B Good, Paul Gulick, Gurer Gundondu, Mary Haber, Steven Hamilton, Katie Heines, Tatiana Irvine, Bonnie Januszewski-Ytuarte, Diane Januszewski, Frank Januszewski, Ellen Johnson, Paul Kalland, Jill Krol, Chris Krueger, Annetta Kushner, Angela Lauria, Judy Lazarus, Christine Lee, Patricia Locke, John Loonam, Lynn MacDougall, Naomi Marsh, Harriett Masembe, Walter Mattson, James McCarron, Susannah McGlamery, Tim Mewmaw, Tara Rose Morrison, Dan Murphy, Pam Murray, Mary-Lynne Neil, Chris Nelson, Julie Olenn, Mark Oshinskie, Suzy Paalman, Chris Pitchford, James Pitchford, Andrew Ranson, Tim Reilly, Marla Sanzone, Nathaniel Torrey, Kathleen Towner, Sharie Valerio, Jan-Willem Van Der Vossen, Taylor Waters, Nicholas Wheeless, Andrew Wildermuth, and Bernadette Zorio.

Jerry Januszewski
Annapolis, Maryland
January 2019

Made in the USA
Columbia, SC
19 February 2019